Sports in America
1920–1939

SECOND EDITION

JAMES BUCKLEY JR.
AND JOHN WALTERS

SERIES FOREWORD BY
LARRY KEITH

CHELSEA HOUSE
PUBLISHERS
An imprint of Infobase Publishing

1920–1939, Second Edition
Sports in America

Chelsea House
An Imprint of Infobase Publishing
132 West 31st Street
New York, NY 10001

Library of Congress Cataloging-in-Publication Data

Walters, John (John Andrew)
  Sports in America, 1920-1939 / John Walters ; series foreword by Larry Keith
    p. cm.
  Includes bibliographical references and index.
  ISBN-13: 978-1-60413-449-0 (hardcover : alk. paper)
  ISBN-10: 1-60413-449-6 (hardcover : alk. paper) 1. Sports—United States—History—20th century. 2. Sports—Social as-
pects—United States—History—20th century. I. Title.

  GV583.W35 2010
  796.09730904—dc22

                                                                                    2009016535

Chelsea House books are available at special discounts when purchased in bulk quantities for businesses,
associations, institutions, or sales promotions. Please call our Special Sales Department in New York at
(212) 967-8800 or (800) 322-8755.

You can find Chelsea House on the World Wide Web at http://www.chelseahouse.com

Produced by the Shoreline Publishing Group LLC
President/Editorial Director: James Buckley Jr.
Contributing Editors: Jim Gigliotti, Beth Adelman
Text design by Thomas Carling, carlingdesign.com
Index by Nanette Cardon, IRIS
Cover printed by Bang Printing, Brainerd, Minn.
Book printed and bound by Bang Printing, Brainerd, Minn.
Date printed: July 2010

Photo credits: AP/Wide World: 11, 14, 19, 22, 30, 31, 39, 40, 43, 44, 47, 49, 52, 53, 54, 57, 58, 63, 65, 69, 75, 81, 85,
86, 89, 90, 93, 94, 95, 97, 99, 101; Courtesy Champions of the Ring: 46; Corbis 7, 8, 9, 15, 72, 103; Pat DeLong:
92; Getty Images: 13, 83, 100, 104; Courtesy Goal Line Art by Gary Thomas: 28, 35; Courtesy Lexington Horse
Park: 12; Library of Congress: 51; National Baseball Library: 20, 21, 32, 41, 43 (inset), 50, 57 (inset), 60, 64, 70,
74, 76, 82, 91, 98, 105; Courtesy Notre Dame Archives: 37; Shoreline Publishing Group: 33, 55, 69 (inset), 73, 81
(inset), 87; Whitney Museum of Art (painting by George Bellows): 25.
  Sports icons by Bob Eckstein.

Printed in the United States of America.

10 9 8 7 6 5 4 3 2 1

This book is printed on acid-free paper.

CONTENTS

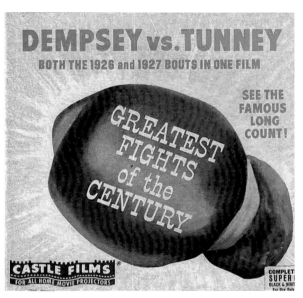

In this "Golden Age of Sports," boxing was one of the biggest attractions. Jack Dempsey and Gene Tunny had two famous battles.

FOREWORD

BY LARRY KEITH

WHEN THE EDITORS OF SPORTS IN AMERICA invited me to write the foreword to this important historical series I recalled my experience in the 1980s as the adjunct professor for a new sports journalism course in the graduate school of Columbia University. Before granting their approval, the faculty at that prestigious Ivy League institution asked, Do sports matter? Are they relevant? Are they more than just fun and games?

The answer—an emphatic yes—is even more appropriate today than it was then. As an integral part of American society, sports provide insights to our history and culture and, for better or worse, help define who we are.

Sports In America is much more than a compilation of names, dates, and facts. Each volume chronicles accomplishments and expansions of the possible. Not just in the physical ability to perform, but in the ability to create goals and determine methods to achieve them. In this way, sports, the sweaty offspring of recreation and competition, resemble any other field of endeavor. I certainly wouldn't equate the race for a gold medal with the race to the moon, but the building blocks are the same: the intelligent application of talent, determination, research, practice, and hard work to a meaningful objective.

Sports matter because they show us in high definition. They communicate examples of determination, courage, and skill. They often embody a heroic human-interest story, overcoming poverty, injustice, injury, or disease. The phrase, "Sports is a microcosm of life," could also read "Life is a microcosm of sport."

Consider racial issues. When Jackie Robinson of the Brooklyn Dodgers broke through major league baseball's "color barrier" in 1947, the significance extended beyond the national pastime. Precisely because baseball was the national pastime, this epochal event reverberated throughout every part of American society.

To be sure, black stars from individual sports had preceded him (notably Joe Louis in boxing and Jesse Owens in track), and others would follow (Arthur Ashe in tennis and Tiger Woods in golf), but Robinson stood out as an important member of a team. He wasn't just playing with the Dodgers, he was traveling with them, living with them. He was a black member of a white athletic family. The benefits of integration could be appreciated far beyond the borough of Brooklyn. In 1997, Major League Baseball retired his "42" jersey number.

Sports have always been a laboratory for social awareness and change. Robinson integrated big league box scores eight years before the U.S. Supreme Court ordered the integration of public schools. The Paralympics (1960) and Special Olympics (1968) easily predate the Americans with Disabilities Act (1990). The mainstreaming of disabled athletes was especially apparent in 2007 when double amputee Jessica Long, 15, won the AAU Sullivan Award as America's top amateur. Women's official debut in the Olympic Games, though limited to swimming, occurred in 1912, seven years before they got the right to vote. So even if these sports were tardy in opening their doors, in another way, they were ahead of their times. And if it was necessary to break down some of those doors—Title IX support for female college athletes comes to mind—so be it. Basketball star Candace Parker won't let anyone keep her from the hoop.

Another area of importance, particularly as it affects young people, is substance abuse. High school, college, and professional teams all oppose the illegal use of drugs, tobacco, and alcohol. In most venues, testing is mandatory, and tolerance is zero. The confirmed use of performance enhancing drugs has damaged the reputations of such superstar athletes as Olympic sprinters Ben Johnson and Marion Jones, cyclist Floyd Landis, and baseball sluggers Manny Ramirez and Alex Rodriguez. Some athletes have lost their careers, or even their lives, to substance abuse. Conversely, other athletes have used their fame to caution young people about submitting to peer pressure or making poor choices.

Fans care about sports and sports personalities because they provide entertainment and self-identify—too often at a loss of priorities. One reason sports have flourished in this country is their support from governmental bodies. When a city council votes to help underwrite the cost of a sports facility or give financial advantages to the owners of a team, it affects the pocketbook of every taxpayer, not to mention the local ecosystem. When high schools and colleges allocate significant resources to athletics, administrators believe they are serving the greater good, but at what cost? Decisions with implications beyond the sports page merit everyone's attention.

In World War II, our country's sporting passion inspired President Franklin Roosevelt to declare that professional games should not be cancelled. He felt the benefits to the national psyche outweighed the risk of gathering large crowds at central locations. In 2001, another generation of Americans also continued to attend large-scale sports events because, to do otherwise, would "let the terrorists win." Being there, being a fan, yelling your lungs out, cheering victory and bemoaning defeat, is a cleansing, even therapeutic exercise. The security check at the gate is just part of the price of stepping inside. Even before there was a 9/11, there was a bloody terrorist assault at the Munich Olympic Games in 1972.

The popular notion "Sports build character" has been better expressed "Sports reveal character." We've witnessed too many coaches and athletes break rules of fair play and good conduct. The convictions of NBA referee Tim Donaghy for gambling and NFL quarterback Michael Vick for operating a dog-fighting ring are startling recent examples. We've even seen violence and cheating in youth sports, often by parents of a (supposed) future superstar. We've watched (at a safe distance) fans "celebrate" championships with destructive behavior. I would argue, however, that these flaws are the exception, not the rule, that the good of sports far outweighs the bad, that many of life's success stories took root on an athletic field.

Any serious examination of sports leads to the question of athletes as standards for conduct. Professional basketball star Charles Barkley created quite a stir in 1993 when he used a Nike shoe commercial to declare, "I am not paid to be a role model." The knee-jerk response argued, "Of course you are, because kids look up to you," but Barkley was right to raise the issue. He was saying that, in making lifestyle choices in language and behavior, young people should look elsewhere for role models, ideally to responsible parents or guardians.

The fact remains, however, that athletes occupy an exalted place in our society, especially when they are magnified in the mass media, sports talk radio, and the blogosphere. The athletes we venerate can be as young as a high school basketball player or as old as a Hall of Famer. (They can even be dead, as Babe Ruth's commercial longevity attests.) They are honored and coddled in a way few mortals are. Regrettably, we can be quick to excuse their excesses and ignore their indulgences. They influence the way we live and think: Ted Williams inspired patriotism as a wartime fighter pilot; Muhammad Ali's opposition to the Vietnam War on religious grounds, validated by the Supreme Court, encouraged the peace movement; Magic Johnson's contraction of the HIV/AIDs virus brought better understanding to a little-understood disease. No wonder we elect them—track stars, football coaches, baseball pitchers—to represent us in Washington. Meanwhile, television networks pay huge sums to sports leagues so their teams can pay fortunes for their services.

Indeed, it has always been this way. If we, as a nation, love sports, then we, quite naturally, will love the men and women who play them best. In return, they provide entertainment, release and inspiration. From the beginning of the 20th century until now, Sports In America is their story-and ours.

Larry Keith is the former Assistant Managing Editor of Sports Illustrated. *He created the editorial concept for* SI Kids *and was the editor of the official Olympic programs in 1996, 2000 and 2002. He is a former adjunct professor of Sports Journalism at Columbia University and is a member of the North Carolina Journalism Hall of Fame.*

INTRODUCTION
1920–1939

MORE THAN A NEW DECADE ARRIVED when the clock struck midnight on December 31, 1919. A new American era dawned, or at least would begin to dawn, just three days later. America woke up on January 1, 1920, unaware of just how much grandeur and spectacle was on the horizon. The preceding decade had been marred by war and scandal, by the worst of what humanity is capable. World War I raged from 1914 to 1919, devastating Europe on a scale never before seen. In the sports world, the conflict forced the cancellation of the Olympics in 1916 and the downsizing of the period's popular team sports, baseball and college football.

Major League Baseball, the only one of today's big three pro sports that existed at the time, had been rocked by the 1919 Black Sox scandal. Eight members of the Chicago White Sox were accused of fixing the World Series that year, that is, intentionally causing the White Sox to lose so that gamblers would benefit. The integrity and future of baseball faced a very dire threat. Then, just three weeks into what would forever be known as The Roaring

Twenties, everything changed. On January 3 the New York Yankees, a team that had never won a World Series, paid the Boston Red Sox a substantial amount of cash in exchange for pitcher and rightfielder George Herman "Babe" Ruth. In the hindsight of destiny, the $125,000 (plus a $385,000 loan) the Yanks paid the Red Sox, who had won four World Series in the 1910s, was the bargain of the century.

Ruth went on to become one of the greatest athletes in a team sport in American history. Ruth was bigger, in size, in feats, and in his appetite for life, than anything anyone had ever seen. He was, quite simply, the perfect symbol of the decade. Only 1980s and 1990s basketball hero Michael Jordan comes close.

Suddenly, athletes and entertainers were rich and famous. They became celebrities. Think quickly: Can you name an American actor, musician, or athlete from before 1920? Can your dad or mom? There were a handful, at best—Jim Thorpe, Ty Cobb, Jack Johnson, athletes all—whose names come to mind. But that's about it.

A Baseball King *Babe Ruth almost single-handedly saved baseball from a scandal.*

Before 1920, politicians, generals, and writers were America's celebrities. The dawn of Ruth, plus a country that suddenly had more leisure time, technology, and wealth than any nation ever, changed all that. The 1920s introduced the world to boxer Jack Dempsey, football coach Knute Rockne, football star Red Grange, and super horse Man O' War—just a few of the heroes readers will meet in this book.

1920–1939

Before 1920, there was no radio and certainly no television. Jazz music was in its infancy. There were a few films, but they had no sound until 1927. Before 1920, in sports, there was no National Football League, no Winter Olympics, no Harlem Globetrotters (the National Basketball Association was decades away from being formed), no All-Star Games in any sport and, just in case you were wondering, no X Games. How thin the sports section of the newspaper must have been back then!

The arrival of Ruth in New York City in 1920 opened the floodgates. That sea-son, the Yankees, who shared a stadium with the New York Giants because Yankee Stadium had not yet been built, became the first Major League team to draw more than 1 million fans. What had always been America's National Pastime suddenly became one of its biggest entertainment successes, too.

That same year a group of men met in an auto showroom in Canton, Ohio, and formed the American Pro Football Association (APFA). Two years later, they changed the name to the National Football League, beginning that league's journey to its position today at the top of the American sports scene.

Later in 1920, Major League Baseball appointed its first commissioner, a former judge named Kenesaw Mountain Landis. The new commissioner would deal with the Black Sox eight harshly, barring them from baseball for life. Whether or not they were guilty was immaterial to Landis; he was acting to save baseball, which he did.

Also in 1920, Prohibition, which made it illegal to manufacture, sell or drink liquor, came into effect. The government may as well have tried to sop up the Great Lakes with a dish towel. These were fast, fun and frantic times. Americans wanted to pop a few champagne corks, both literally and figuratively. It was a decade when a song called "Ain't We Got Fun" became a hit, and no title better defined the times.

The times were intoxicating. So men created football leagues and built huge stadiums, such as Yankee Stadium and the Los Angeles Coliseum and the Rose Bowl, to name just a few. They staged colossal heavyweight fights with $1

Down the Drain *From 1920 to 1929, it was illegal to make, sell, or drink liquor in the United States. Local officials, as here in Chicago, poured out millions of gallons of alcoholic beverages, such as beer.*

million in prize money and swam across the English Channel (actually, a woman did that, too, and faster than the men!) and flew airplanes across the Atlantic Ocean and even won one for the Gipper (see page 13).

It was left to a writer, the voice of that age, to sum it up best. "Here was a new generation," wrote novelist F. Scott Fitzgerald, "dedicated more than the last to the fear of poverty and the worship of success; grown up to find all gods dead, all wars fought, all faiths in man shaken."

Not everyone participated in the new riches of the sports world. African-Americans were still banned from playing professional baseball and none played pro football. Some colleges offered black athletes a place to play, but the opportunities were limited.

Women, too, had only minor roles to play in the wide world of sports in the era. There were no women's pro sports and few colleges offered sports for female students. The Olympics were one of the

Singing Out Loud *Al Jolson (right) starred in* The Jazz Singer, *the first motion picture with sound. It was released in 1927 and marked a new era in American entertainment.*

few venues where women could earn a share of the athletic glory.

By the end of the decade, Babe Ruth was earning more than the President of the United States. "Why not?" said the Babe. "I had a better year than he did." Sports, finally and forever, arrived to stake its claim to America's heart and soul.

1920

Curse of the Bambino

The Roaring Twenties flew out of the starting gate. On January 3 the Boston Red Sox sold the best baseball player of all time, George Herman "Babe" Ruth (1895–1948), to the New York Yankees.

In 1920 the Yankees were a 17-year-old team that had never won a pennant. The Red Sox had won four World Series in the past eight seasons. Ruth, only 24, had already led the American League in home runs or tied for the lead in the past two seasons. But Red Sox owner Harry Frazee, who was also a theatrical producer, was riddled with debt. He desperately needed money to finance his new Broadway show, *No! No! Nanette.* In a deal that has haunted Boston baseball fans ever since, Frazee sold Ruth to New York for $100,000 in cash and a $385,000 loan.

The Yankees immediately doubled Ruth's salary—at his demand—to a then unheard-of $20,000 a year. No athlete had ever been paid so much. But the Babe was worth every penny. In his first season with the Yankees, Ruth hit 54 home runs. By July 19 he had already broken his own single-season record of 29 homers, set the year before.

Ruthian: There was no other word to describe the Babe's extraordinary feats. No other major league *team* hit as many homers as Ruth did in 1920. He also had an .847 slugging percentage (the total number of bases gained on all base hits, divided by the number of times a player has been at bat). Ruth's slugging record lasted until Barry Bonds broke it in 2002. He was primarily responsible for the Yankees becoming the first Major League ball club to draw more than 1 million fans (1,289,422) in a single season.

The only thing Ruth failed to do in his first season in New York was lead the Yankees to the league title. Instead, the Cleveland Indians represented the American League in the World Series. The Indians, aided by second baseman Bill Wambsganss's unassisted triple play (still the only one in World Series play), beat the Brooklyn Dodgers in seven games.

Still, the sale of Ruth became the single most important—and infamous—deal in sports history. It dramatically reversed the World Series fortunes of both teams. The Yankees would win 26 World Series through the end of the 2008 season. The "cursed" Red Sox didn't win a title again until 2004.

GEORGE HERMAN
(BABE) RUTH

BIG LEAGUE CHEWING GUM

A Heck of a Hitter *Baseball cards were already a big part of many fans' experience of baseball by the time this Babe Ruth card came out in 1920.*

Man O' War

The first time jockey Johnny Loftus attempted to climb aboard Man O' War, the two-year-old colt tossed him nearly 40 feet. "Tossing Johnny," remarked the horse's owner, Samuel Riddle, "was the last bad move Man O' War ever made."

The chestnut thoroughbred was the stuff of legend. In June of 1919, he got his first victory in his very first start, a six-length win at Belmont Park in New York.

1920

He won the next six races he entered, as well, before losing by a half-length to a horse ironically named Upset.

Man O' War entered 1920 as a three year-old with nine victories and one defeat. He would have been a shoo-in to win the Triple Crown (the Kentucky Derby, Preakness and Belmont Stakes races) except that his owner disapproved of three-year-olds running the mile-and-a-quarter Kentucky Derby in early May, which is early in the racing season. But Man O' War did win the Preakness Stakes and the Belmont Stakes—by 20 lengths.

Man O' War's lone rival was Sir Barton, a horse who had won the Triple Crown one year earlier. At a time when horse racing was as popular as any other sport in the country, these two magnificent animals were head and shoulders above the rest of the field. But which was better? No one knew, since they had never raced against each other.

On October 12 the two legends were pitted against one another in a match race (only those two horses were entered) at Kenilworth Park in Windsor, Ontario. The prize was grand for that time: $80,000.

As it turned out, there was no doubt. Man O' War defeated Sir Barton by seven lengths. He was retired afterward, having won 20 of 21 races in his career.

A Brand New League

Full-time professional football was born in 1920. While there had been brief attempts to start pro leagues in the past, this was the one that stuck. A group of team owners gathered in a Hupmobile (the Toyota of its day) showroom in Canton, Ohio. They formed the American Professional Football Association. Needing a "name" to attract press attention, they brought in Olympic champion Jim Thorpe as the league president. Thorpe actually didn't do much of anything presidential, but he was still a top player

Fourteen teams took part in that first season. All but one of the teams was from Illinois, Ohio, or Indiana. The Akron Pros were named the first champion of the new league with an 8–0–3 record. They were led by Fritz Pollard, the first African-American coach in the league.

You say you've never heard of the ol' APFA? Perhaps you know them better by the name they took on starting in 1922: The National Football League (NFL).

One in a Million *A statue of the great Man O' War stands at Lexington Horse Park in Kentucky, a national horseracing hotbed.*

Other Milestones of 1920

✔ On February 13 in Kansas City, Missouri, Rube Foster founded the Negro National League. The first financially successful blacks-only baseball league, the Negro National League spawned dozens of similar leagues over the next three decades.

✔ Bill Tilden became the first American to win a singles tennis title at Wimbledon. Later that summer, Tilden won the first of six straight U.S. Open singles championships. "Big" Bill became the first male tennis star to gain national notice.

"Big" Bill Tilden

✔ The Summer Olympics returned to the sports calendar and were held in Antwerp, Belgium. The Games of 1916 had been cancelled due to World War I. The United States captured 41 medals. Sprinter Charles Paddock was the first to earn the title "World's Fastest Human" by winning the 100-meter race. Hawaiian swimmer Duke Kahanamoku, also a surfing pioneer set a world record in the 100-meter freestyle. Italian fencer Nedo Nadi proved unbeatable, winning five gold medals while dominating every form of the sport.

The Gipper

In 1920 the University of Notre Dame football team compiled its second consecutive 9–0 season. The little Catholic school in northern Indiana was beginning to make a name for itself, thanks primarily to its All-American halfback, George Gipp (1895–1920).

Gipp was one of the game's greatest all-around players. As a freshman, he drop-kicked a game-winning 62-yard field goal. In four seasons, he scored 83 touchdowns for the Fighting Irish.

Gipp almost did not get to play his senior year. He was voted team captain, but was expelled from school for missing too many law classes. Gipp begged his coach, Knute Rockne (1888–1931) to convince the law professors to give him an oral exam. They agreed that if Gipp could prove he knew all the material, he would be reinstated. He easily passed the exam.

The Fighting Irish were trailing Indiana, 10–7, late in the seventh game of the season. Gipp, who had broken his collarbone earlier in the game, scored the winning touchdown on a five-yard run.

The following Saturday, November 20, Notre Dame played at Northwestern University. Ordered not to run because of the collarbone injury, Gipp instead threw a 55-yard touchdown pass, the final one of his career. Notre Dame won, 33–7.

The Fighting Irish capped their undefeated season with a 25–0 Thanksgiving Day win against Michigan State. Gipp did not play. He had contracted a strep infection on the day of the Northwestern game. Nineteen days later, he was dead. His strep infection had led to a fatal bout of pneumonia. On December 14 Notre Dame's first and most mythic All-American died in a hospital bed at the age of 25. In 1928 (see page 50), Gipp's legend rose again and assumed a permanent place in sports (and, later, political) history.

1921

The Original Celtics

On April 16 more than 11,000 basketball fans jammed the 71st Street Armory in Manhattan. They came to watch a one-day, best-of-three basketball "World Series" between the New York Original Celtics and the New York Whirlwinds.

Most of the Original Celtics (so-called because the name New York Celtics was taken by another team; the 1923 version is shown below), including gritty 5-foot-10 guard John Beckman, hailed from Manhattan's Hell's Kitchen neighborhood. Beckman was known as "the Babe Ruth of basketball." He was an outstanding free throw shooter at a time when one player was permitted to attempt all of his team's free throws.

In the opener, Beckman scored 25 points, 23 on free throws, in a losing effort. The Whirlwinds won 40–27. In the second game, Beckman was again the high scorer, netting 17 points in a 26–24 victory. Fans were in a frenzy waiting for the third and deciding game to begin—perhaps too much of a frenzy. Officials inside the Armory feared the mood had gone from enthusiastic to violent, and they canceled the third game.

The Original Celtics were basketball's first great national team. A permanent professional league was not founded until 1948, and traveling teams like the Celtics were the class of what was still a very young sport—basketball had been invented only 30 years earlier.

The team known today as the Boston Celtics of the NBA took its name from this barnstorming early club.

What a Team! *Note the heavy leather knee pads worn by the members of the Original Celtics basketball team. Players also wore heavy wool jerseys in these days before synthetic materials.*

Ten-Goal Tommy *Tommy Hitchcock, the greatest American polo player of all time.*

America's Polo Legend

The sport of polo, in which four players on each team advance a ball with a mallet while riding horses called polo ponies, was very popular in the 1920s. Polo's top international match, the West-chester Cup between the United States and Great Britain, had resumed after being suspended due to World War I.

1921

Tommy Hitchcock was the United States' top polo player and a war hero as well. As a pilot, he had been shot down over Germany and taken prisoner. Hitchcock, only 18 at the time, had jumped from a prisoner-of-war train and walked 100 miles to Switzerland and freedom.

Now, in London in June, playing in front of Britain's King George V and Prime Minister Winston Churchill, Hitchcock was similarly bold and impressive. In the first game in what would be a 2–0 United States sweep, Hitchcock outscored the entire British side.

Hitchcock was so well-known among the high-living polo set that author F. Scott Fitzgerald supposedly modeled the character Tom Buchanan in *The Great Gatsby* after Hitchcock.

Dempsey KOs Carpentier

Jersey City, New Jersey, was home to the most anticipated heavyweight championship match in years, pitting the champ, American Jack Dempsey, against Frenchman Georges Carpentier.

No fight had ever promised such fanfare—or cash. Promoter Tex Rickard paid $250,000 for a stadium to be built and promised Dempsey himself $300,000. It was money well spent. When the opening bell rang two months later, on July 2, the fight became the first in history to earn $1 million on ticket sales.

On the day of the fight, 80,183 spectators filed into the arena. "Did you ever see so many millionaires?" asked Rickard, who himself was one. The bell saved

The End of the Fix

Baseball fans were preoccupied all summer long with what was known as the Black Sox Scandal. A year earlier, a Chicago grand jury had indicted eight players from the Chicago White Sox for conspiring to fix (lose on purpose in return for money) the 1919 World Series. Gamblers paid the players to lose the games; with this knowledge, the gamblers could make lots of money by placing bets against the White Sox.

The Black Sox Scandal threatened to undermine the sport's integrity. In response, Major League Baseball appointed federal judge Kenesaw Mountain Landis to be its first commissioner. Landis's job was to restore faith in America's national pastime.

"Baseball is something more than a game to an American boy," said Landis upon his appointment. "It is his training field for life work. Destroy his faith in its squareness and honesty, and you have destroyed something more; you have planted suspicion of all things in his heart."

The trial for the eight White Sox players, including Chicago's outstanding centerfielder, "Shoeless" Joe Jackson, began in July, 1921. On August 2, a grand jury found the eight White Sox players innocent of all charges.

The players' innocence in the eyes of the law did not change Landis' mind. That evening, he banned all eight men from baseball for life. The debate about his actions, especially concerning Jackson, one of the game's greatest all-time hitters, continues to this day, with some calling for Jackson's name to be cleared.

Other Milestones of 1921

✔ Charles Paddock, the reigning Olympic gold medalist in the 100-meter race, was still a student at the University of Southern California when the track team traveled north to Berkeley for an April 23 meet. That afternoon, he set four world records, in the 100-, 200-, and 300-meter races, as well as in the 300-yard sprint.

✔ On the ice, the Ottawa Senators won their second consecutive Stanley Cup and National Hockey League championship.

✔ Bill Tilden again won both the Wimbledon and U.S. Open singles tennis titles.

✔ The football team from tiny Centre College in Danville, Kentucky, defeated mighty Harvard 6–0 on October 29, ending Harvard's 23-game winning streak.

Dempsey in round two and did the same for Carpentier in round three (that is, the fighters were knocked down just as the bell rang to end those rounds).

In the fourth, Dempsey knocked the Frenchman to the canvas, and blood spurted from Carpentier's mouth.

In New York's Times Square, a loudspeaker described the live result to an anxious throng of boxing fans: "Carpentier makes no effort to rise . . . The fight is over! Jack Dempsey remains heavyweight champion of the world!"

The following morning *The New York Times* devoted one front-page column to the news that President Warren G. Harding had signed a peace treaty officially ending World War I. On the same page the *Times* devoted five columns and a three-level headline to the Dempsey-Carpentier fight.

Giants Win Series

The New York Yankees ran away from the rest of the American League. Outfielder Babe Ruth set new marks for home runs (59) and runs batted in (170) in a season, while batting .378.

In the National League, the New York Giants rode the hitting of infielders Frankie Frisch and George Kelly to the pennant. New York baseball fans enjoyed a Polo Grounds World Series. This was the first time that all the World Series games were played at one stadium.

This World Series was the last best-of-nine series in Major League Baseball history. It was also the first to be broadcast on radio. The Giants, who won the World Series in 1905 before losing their next four trips to the Fall Classic, rallied from a two-games-to-none deficit to beat the Yankees five games to three.

1922

Mr. DeMar-athon

On April 19 in Boston, Clarence DeMar won his first Boston Marathon in 11 years. The marathon distance was then 24.5 miles, and DeMar covered the distance in a course-record 2:18.10. Two years later, all marathon courses adopted the current standard 26.2-mile distance.

DeMar, whose first win at Boston came in 1911, routinely ran 100 miles per week. "Mr. DeMar-athon" eventually won five more Boston Marathons—with his last victory coming in 1930 at the age of 41. His record of seven Boston victories is unlikely to be equaled.

A Watery Tarzan

On June 23 in Honolulu, swimmer Johnny Weissmuller (1904–1984) caused a sensation. Just 17 years old, the Illinois lad broke four freestyle world swimming records at distances of 300 and 400 meters and 440 and 500 yards. As great as this day was, the future Olympic gold-medal winner and star of Tarzan movies still had his best days in the pool ahead of him (see page 33).

Basketball Barnstormers

The New York Original Celtics, the best team of basketball talent the sport had yet seen, took off on a 205-game national tour. Until then, the Original Celtics, with such future Hall of Famers as John Beckman, Dutch Dehnert, and Nat Holman, had played most of their games at Manhattan's Central Opera House. But this year the Cagers—so called because chicken wire surrounded the court to protect spectators from errant passes—took their act on the road. The Original Celtics dominated, going 193–11–1.

Uptown, in Harlem, another barnstorming basketball team was being formed. A Caribbean immigrant named Bob Douglas had the idea to form an all-black team. He named them the Renaissance after their home court, the Renaissance Casino and Ballroom, on the corner of 138th Street and 7th Avenue. The Rens did not play their first game until the following year.

Decades later, Douglas, known as "the Father of Black Basketball," became the first African American enshrined in the Basketball Hall of Fame.

From Pool to Jungle *Johnny Weissmuller moved on from being one of the most successful American swimmers in history to playing Tarzan in a series of movies.*

Hornsby and Sisler Light Up St. Louis

The highlight of the baseball season came in St. Louis, Missouri, where a pair of future Hall of Fame players put on a great batting show.

Like the New York Giants and New York Yankees, the St. Louis Browns (American League) and St. Louis Cardinals (National League) occupied the same stadium, Sportsman's Park. The Browns had left-handed hitter George Sisler (1893–1973), most likely the sec-

1922

Sweet Swinger *The outstanding Rogers Hornsby is among the best righthanded hitters of all time.*

game hit streak. Despite all this, Williams did not receive a single vote for A.L. Most Valuable Player. Sisler was simply too spectacular.

Sisler, who had an engineering degree from the University of Michigan, batted an astounding .420 and led the major leagues in stolen bases with 51. An outstanding fielder, Sisler's 41-game hit streak helped the Browns come within one game of wresting the pennant away from the Yankees. Sisler was, in the words of baseball great Ty Cobb, "the nearest thing to a perfect ballplayer."

If Sisler was the nearest thing to perfection, where did that put Hornsby? The Rajah, as he was known, won baseball's Triple Crown, leading the National League in batting average (.401), RBI (152) and home runs (42). Only Babe Ruth, who began the season serving a 40-day suspension for playing in exhibition games during the off season, had ever whacked that many homers in a single season.

A Busy Baseball Season

Detroit Tigers outfielder Ty Cobb batted .399 or .401, depending on whom you asked. Cobb, who still holds the record for highest career batting average (.367; Hornsby is second at .358), initially fell one hit short of his third .400 season. At season's end, he had 210 base hits in 526 at-bats for a .39924 average. However, it was recalled that Cobb, then 35 years old, had reached base in a May 15 game against the Yankees on a controversial error. Cobb hit a line drive, which ricocheted off Yankees third baseman Deacon Scott's glove.

ond-best first baseman (behind Lou Gehrig) of all time. The Cardinals countered with second baseman Rogers Hornsby (1896–1963), considered perhaps the best ever at his position.

How good a season did both Sisler and Hornsby have? Sisler's teammate, leftfielder Ken Williams, led the American League in home runs (39) and runs batted in (RBI, 155). Williams also became the first 30–30 player (30 homers, 30 stolen bases) in Major League history, as well as the first American Leaguer to homer three times in a game, and he had a 28-

At the time, a moderate rain had begun at the Polo Grounds and official scorer John Kieran scurried for cover under a distant grandstand. Fred Lieb, a writer who remained in the press box, called it a hit. Kieran, though, called it an error even though he was in poor position to see the play.

A controversy brewed. Finally, A.L. president Ban Johnson overruled Kieran's call, awarding Cobb the hit some five months after the play. Thus the Georgia Peach, as Cobb was nicknamed, had 211 hits, giving him a .401 average. Cobb became the first player in the 20th century to have three .400 seasons.

Cobb's post-season base hit was one of many oddities in baseball this year. On August 25, the Chicago Cubs nearly blew a 19-run lead, hanging on to defeat the Philadelphia Phillies, 26–23. The two teams set a record that still stands for most runs scored in one game.

Meanwhile, the Supreme Court weighed in on the national pastime, ruling that baseball was "sport" and not "commerce" and therefore not subject to antitrust laws. The landmark ruling has affected the manner in which Major League Baseball conducts its "sport" ever since. The ruling still allows Major League Baseball to make rules for its entire sport from a central office, even though each team is supposedly an independent business. This central office can make decisions for the teams without regard to antitrust laws that govern other businesses in the United States. As recently as the 1990s, this decision has been affirmed by Congress and the courts in several decisions and bills.

Princeton Tackles Chicago

The nationwide popularity of college football continued to grow, helped by some new technology.

On October 28 the University of Chicago hosted Princeton University in a battle of unbeaten teams. Radio station WEAF of New York aired the game from coast to coast—the first such football broadcast. Chicago, a football powerhouse coached by Amos Stagg, was heavily favored. As expected, Chicago led through three quarters, 18–7, thanks to three touchdowns by fullback John Thomas.

The Weird Series

The season's odd twists and turns took baseball right back to where it had been the previous October. Once again, the Giants and Yankees met at the Polo Grounds, this time in a best-of-seven series. The Yankees, who had already announced they were moving into a new stadium across the Harlem River in the Bronx next year, bid their Polo Grounds hosts a rude farewell. Despite Babe Ruth batting only .118 and going without a home run, the Yanks swept the Giants 4–0.

In fact, there was another game that ended in a tie. With the sun still shining brightly one afternoon, officials called the game "on account of darkness." An irate baseball commissioner Kenesaw Landis, suspecting that the Giants and Yanks were trying to extend the series (and, hence, make more money from ticket sales; an actual ticket is pictured here), donated that game's receipts to charity.

1922

However, before a stunned crowd in Chicago, the Princeton Tigers roared back in the fourth quarter, scoring touchdowns on a 40-yard fumble return and a fourth-down, goal-line plunge. Then the game came down to one key play. Chicago, trailing 21–18, drove to the Princeton one-yard line. On fourth down, the Chicago Maroons handed the ball to Thomas, who was tackled by Princeton's Harland "Pink" Baker for no gain. Nobody had blocked Baker. In a huge upset, Princeton won the game.

"There was so much yelling and screaming going on," recalled another Princeton defender, "that Chicago's linemen didn't shift properly." Chicago's hometown advantage had disappeared in a cloud of noise.

Woman with a Gun *Annie Oakley broke gender barriers (along with a lot of targets) with her incredible sharpshooting skills.*

Annie Oakley Hangs Up Her Pistols

Annie Oakley, whose sharpshooting had made her the star of Buffalo Bill Cody's Wild West Show decades earlier, hung up her six-shooters at the age of 62. She did so with, appropriately, a bang. On April 16 in Pinehurst, North Carolina, Annie got her gun for a trapshooting demonstration. Showing no signs of diminishing skills, she hit 100 clay targets in a row.

Two Unbeaten Seasons

In Ithaca in upstate New York, "Gloomy" Gil Dobie, the football coach at Cornell University, was forging the 13th unbeaten season of his illustrious career. Dobie, who never lost a game in nine years as head coach at the University of Washington and two at North Dakota State before that, was in his third season at Cornell. With All-American Eddie Kaw leading the charge, Cornell's Big Red enjoyed their second straight undefeated season with Dobie.

A few hours east of Ithaca, at the U.S. Military Academy at West Point, Army coach Charles Daly was putting the finishing touches on a unique career. Daly had played for both Harvard University and Army in the previous century—he is the only person to play on a Harvard team that beat Yale and an Army team that beat Navy. Those two matchups are among the oldest and fiercest rivalries in college sports. In Daly's final season as coach at West Point, he led the Cadets to an undefeated season.

Other Milestones of 1922

✔ Babe Ruth was suspended five different times during the season for, among other matters, barnstorming (playing non-approved games), throwing dirt in an umpire's face, and attacking a fan in the stands.

✔ Golfer Glenna Collett Vare won the first of a record six U.S. Amateur titles. Today, the LPGA's Vare Trophy for lowest scoring average is named for her.

✔ Golfer Gene Sarazen became the first man to win both the U.S. Open and the Professional Golfers' Association (PGA) titles in the same year.

✔ Bodybuilder Charles Atlas won the "World's Most Perfectly Developed Man" contest at New York City's Madison Square Garden.

✔ Pillory won the Preakness and Belmont Stakes, two-thirds of horse racing's Triple Crown, and is named Horse of the Year.

Welcome, Women!

Women did not take part in sports in nearly the numbers they do today. They were only allowed to hold a handful of events at the Summer Olympics, and weren't thought capable of running events longer than 400 meters. In the Winter Olympics, they could do figure skating, but not skiing (that didn't start until 1936). However, this year, the Amateur Athletic Union recognized officially that women could play a bigger role. For the first time, they organized and held women's events in their many track & field competitions. They still didn't think women could run very far, however—only sprint. Small steps indeed.

1923

Yankee Stadium Opens

On April 18 Babe Ruth and the New York Yankees moved into their brand new ballpark in the Bronx. Yankee Stadium, also known as The House that Ruth Built, was fittingly christened with a 4–1 victory over the Boston Red Sox. As if following a script, Ruth clobbered a game-winning three-run homer against his old team (see page 10) in front of 74,200 gleeful fans. As many as 25,000 more fans were turned away at the gates.

The Giants and Yankees now occupied separate residences, but they still held joint custody of the World Series. For the third consecutive year, both New York teams met in the Fall Classic. Ruth, atoning for the previous October's abysmal performance when he batted .118 in the World Series, hit two home runs in game two and another in the Series-clinching game six.

It was just another Ruthian season at the plate for the Bambino, who came as close as at any time in his career to achieving baseball's Triple Crown. Ruth led the American League in both home runs (41) and RBI (131). As for batting average, the Babe hit a career-best .398, but finished second to Harry Heilmann of the Detroit Tigers. The Detroit outfielder hit .403.

The Yankees might have swept the series were it not for the Giants' Casey Stengel, who hit not one but two game-winning home runs. Stengel won game one with an inside-the-park-home run. Stengel rounded the bases furiously, losing a shoe in the process. His other game-winning shot was a more conventional, over-the-fence hit in game three. As Stengel rounded the bases, he made insulting gestures to his opponents. Decades later, Stengel would manage the Yanks to seven World Series titles.

Jones Wins U.S. Open

Stengel's polar opposite in comportment was a gentleman who swung at a smaller white ball and hit it farther. Pleasant yet reserved, Bobby Jones, Atlanta's favorite son, was a self-taught golfer and played his entire career as an amateur. This year, after four rounds of U.S. Open play, Jones was tied with Bobby Cruickshank.

Though only 21 and a student at Georgia Tech, Jones's road to his first

Out of the Ring *This painting shows Firpo (in purple) knocking eventual winner Dempsey from the ring.*

major win must have seemed long. In 1921 at the British Open, he was so frustrated by his score of 46 after nine holes in the third round that he uncharacteristically tore up his scorecard and walked off the course. Then, in 1922, he lost the U.S. Open to Gene Sarazen by one stroke. Now, on July 15, he was facing 18 more arduous holes against Cruickshank.

Displaying an even temper that would be a hallmark of his career, Jones defeated Cruickshank by two strokes. Who knew

then that it would be only the first of 13 major tournaments that Jones would win in the next eight years—all before his 29th birthday?

Dempsey KOs Firpo

On September 14 heavyweight world champion Jack Dempsey met Argentine challenger Luis Firpo ("The Wild Bull of the Pampas") in front of a sold-out crowd of 90,000 at the Polo Grounds in

1923

New York City. Whereas Dempsey had outweighed challenger Georges Carpentier by 25 pounds in their heavyweight match two years earlier (see page 16), this time the champ was 25 pounds lighter than his opponent.

"They're two big guys," remarked sportswriter Jack Lawrence before he took his ringside seat with the other writers who were covering the fight. "If somebody goes through the ropes [toward us], I hope it's Dempsey. At least he's lighter than that truck Firpo."

Both fighters came out brawling from the bell. Dempsey slipped as he left his corner, and Firpo knocked him down within the first five seconds. The Manassa Mauler, as Dempsey was known, quickly recovered, knocking Firpo down seven times in the first round. Dempsey, ignoring pre-fight instructions to retreat to a neutral corner after a knockdown, simply walloped Firpo each time the Wild Bull got to his feet.

Firpo finally learned his lesson. After the seventh knockdown, the Argentine anticipated Dempsey's onslaught and got the champ on the chin with a screaming right. Dempsey, lifted off his feet, crashed through the ropes—and onto Lawrence's typewriter. Dempsey clambered back into the ring at the count of nine, just before the bell rang ending round one.

The fight included nine knockdowns in its first three minutes. Dempsey, who had been knocked down twice, was reeling. "I was seeing double," he said. "When the bell rang, I went out and hit every Firpo I saw."

Fifty-seven seconds into round two, it was over. Dempsey at last knocked Firpo down and out. Dempsey later called it the "toughest fight I ever had," while many ringside observers believed they had just witnessed "the greatest fight in the history of pugilism," as the *New York Times* reported. In 1950, the *Associated Press* voted the Dempsey–Firpo fight the most dramatic sports event of the half century.

Senators Win Third Stanley Cup

As one dynasty began on the golf course with Bobby Jones, another was nearing its end in the hockey rink. The Ottawa Senators, winners of the Stanley Cup in 1920 and 1921, won their third Cup in four seasons. Offensively, the Senators were paced by right winger Jack Darragh, who would die the following season from acute peritonitis.

No skater meant more to the Senators than goalie Clint Benedict, though. From 1919 to 1923, he led the NHL in lowest goals-against average (the average number of goals scored against his team per game). Only one goalie since (Jacques Plante of the Montreal Canadiens) has equaled Benedict's record. Known as "the praying goaltender" because he spent so much time on his knees in goal, Benedict was the cornerstone of a franchise that was owned by *Ottawa Citizen* sports editor Tommy Gorman.

Ottawa's short mastery of the NHL was waning (the Senators would win one more Stanley Cup this century, in 1927) as Foster Hewitt's began. The son of the sports editor of the *Toronto Star*, Hewitt became the first person to broadcast a hockey game. On March 15, with a scant few hours' notice, Hewitt was assigned to provide a play-by-play account of a play-off game between the Kitchener and Toronto Parkdale teams at the Mutual Street Arena in Toronto. He did the broadcast using an ordinary telephone, cramped inside an improvised four-foot-square glass booth at ice level. The game went into three periods of overtime and the broadcast lasted three hours.

Only 19 and with no one to model himself after, Hewitt shined in his debut. He went on to broadcast some 3,000 hockey games during the next 50 years. He is credited with introducing the famous hockey phrase, "He shoots—he scores!"

Soccer? Here?

Though it was well below the radar of most sports fans in the U.S., the sport of soccer did enjoy a healthy success among some immigrant communities. Cities such as St. Louis and New York, which boasted large numbers of people from Europe, played host to large and popular leagues.

The American Soccer League had eight teams, the most powerful of which was sponsored by Bethlehem Steel, though the J&P Coats team from Pawtucket, Rhode Island, won this season's league title.

More than 115 teams took part in the nationwide U.S. Open Cup. On April 1, the Patterson Silk Sox and Scullin Steel of St. Louis played to a 2–2 tie and were declared co-champions. The success of the event that year led to organizers split-ting the tournament into professional and amateur divisions in 1924.

With the first World Cup of soccer still 15 years away and more traditional "American" sports dominating the head-lines, soccer still had gained a solid foot-hold in America by the 1920s.

The Year in Nonsense

Nonsense caught America's fancy in 1923, a year in which fads such as marathon dancing and flagpole sitting swept the nation and the country's top movie star was a German Shepherd dog named Rin Tin Tin. A year earlier, Syracuse University had banned dancing; now University of Notre Dame coach Knute Rockne was requiring his players to take dancing lessons.

The Philadelphia Athletics lost 20 straight games, tying the Major League Baseball record for futility set by . . . the 1916 Philadelphia Athletics.

No-hit? That was hardly the problem on September 5, when flyweights Gene LaRue and "Kid" Pancho met in the boxing ring. LaRue's hard left to Pancho's jaw was countered simultaneously by the Kid. Both fighters fell to the canvas. Both were counted out by the referee.

Nothing made less sense than a light-heavyweight title match between light-heavyweight champion Mike McTigue, 31, and challenger Willie "Young" Stribling, 19. McTigue, in search of an easy victory, vastly underestimated Stribling's skills.

Pioneer Player *Quarterback/coach Fritz Pollard guided the Akron Pros to the first APFA (later NFL) championship. After 1926, he was the last African-American player in the league until after World War II.*

center of the ring afterward. Alas, the champ's manager, Joe Jacobs, was an influential man. Within three hours Jacobs, by means undetermined, persuaded Ertle to nullify his verdict and declare the fight a draw. Thus, McTigue retained his light-heavyweight world title. In the history of boxing, Stribling's three hours stands as the shortest reign for a world champion.

Photo Opportunity

Finally, there was Zev. On November 17 at Churchill Downs, the Kentucky Derby and Belmont Stakes winner was pitted in a match race against In Memoriam. Zev had already overtaken Man O' War as the all-time money winner among three-year-old horses, with $272,008 in 14 starts (winning 12 of those races).

On this afternoon the 40,000 or so spectators witnessed a photo finish. So close was the race that no winner was declared for a few moments afterward. Then Zev was given the nod. The following day, a slow-motion film appeared to show that In Memoriam had nosed out Zev.

A controversy erupted. The photo finish was still a novelty, and a number of horsemen (and, surely, bettors) did not accept the camera's viewpoint. Zev remained the winner and photo finish cameras would not be regularly used at race tracks for another 13 years.

A Pioneering Pro

When Fritz Pollard was a running back at Brown University, he would dress for games in a cigar store and take a taxi to the games. So hostile were fans

Although McTigue avoided being knocked down all fight long, the consensus among ringside observers was that the challenger had won. Referee Harry Ertle agreed, raising Stribling's arm in triumph when both fighters met in the

Other Milestones of 1923

✔ The Philadelphia Athletics were no-hit twice within a four-day span. The Yankees' Sam Jones no-hit the Phillies on September 4, and the Red Sox Howard Ehmke duplicated the feat on September 7.

✔ The NFL's Canton Bulldogs, led by player-coach Guy Chamberlin, capped off their second consecutive undefeated season.

✔ Because he had already received one college degree (in engineering from Georgia Tech in 1920), Bobby Jones couldn't play golf for Harvard as he pursued a second degree, this time in literature. So he volunteered as the school golf team's assistant manager, though he was the reigning U.S. Open champion!

✔ With matching records of 8–0 and not having played each other, the Universities of Michigan and Illinois each were named college football's national champion by competing governing bodies.

---

toward Pollard, an African-American, that he would wait until just a few minutes before kickoff to take the field. "But I just kept scoring touchdowns," Pollard said, "and that quieted them down."

Pollard was a true gridiron pioneer in the realm of African-American advancement in the sport. As a college player, he was the first black All-American (1915) and in that season scored 10 touchdowns for Brown University, located in Providence, Rhode Island. He was later the first African-American to play in the Rose Bowl (1916; Brown lost to Washington State).

In 1920 he joined the Akron Pros of the fledgling American Pro Football Association (APFA) and became the first black quarterback. Pollard led the Pros to the championship that season as they posted an 8–0–3 record. The following year, Pollard became coach of the Pros. He was the first black head coach in pro football history. He played for the Pros as well, which was common at that time.

From 1922, when the APFA renamed itself the NFL, until 1926, Pollard continued to both play and be a head coach. The Pros finished only 1–6 in 1923 and never repeated their initial success.

Pollard later coached the Milwaukee Badgers and Hammond Pros before rejoining the Akron Pros. After Pollard retired, more than 60 years passed before another African American (Art Shell of the Los Angeles Raiders) was named the head coach of an NFL team. Though Pollard had great success, it was also not until 1950 that a black athlete even played in the NFL.

1924

The Galloping Ghost

October 18, 1924, is probably one of the most important days in college football history. On one spectacular afternoon, the Galloping Ghost and the Four Horsemen rode into immortality.

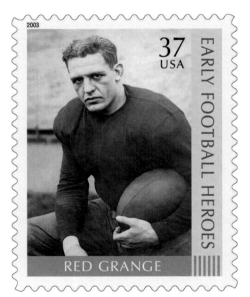

A Ghost of a Stamp *Red Grange was one of four early football heroes honored by the U.S. Postal Service on stamps issued in 2003.*

Speedy University of Illinois halfback Harold "Red" Grange, also known as "The Galloping Ghost," led his team into battle against mighty Michigan. In the days before the game, Grange was just a detail. Both teams had gone 8–0 the previous season. The Michigan Wolverines had not lost since 1921 and had not yet been scored upon this season. As 66,609 fans filed in for the formal dedication of Illinois Memorial Stadium, they expected to see an epic battle. Instead, they witnessed the greatest individual performance the sport had ever seen.

Grange fielded the opening kickoff and returned it 95 yards for a touchdown. Following a Wolverine fumble, he ran 67 yards to score another touchdown. Soon after, Grange scored on a zig-zagging run, dodging defenders for 54 yards. After another Michigan fumble, Grange took a handoff and ran 44 yards into the end zone.

The game was 12 minutes old, and Illinois led 27–0 on Grange's four touchdowns. That was the same number of touchdowns the Wolverines had surrendered all of the last two seasons. "I need a breather," Grange reportedly told his quarterback after his fourth score.

Four Horsemen *This quartet of Notre Dame players became famous thanks to one sportswriter's imagination.*

In the second half, Grange ran 13 yards for a fifth touchdown and passed 20 yards to help account for a sixth. The final score: Illinois 39, Michigan 14. Grange accounted for 402 yards of total offense, including 64 yards passing.

"He is three or four men rolled into one," eminent sportswriter Damon Runyon wrote afterward. "He is Jack Dempsey, Babe Ruth, Al Jolson, Paavo Nurmi, and Man O' War."

The Four Horsemen

On the same day as Grange's breakout success, at the Polo Grounds in New York, another pair of undefeated college football teams, Army and Notre Dame, were playing. Just 10 days earlier, Notre Dame coach Knute Rockne had confided to a friend that his squad was "anything but good . . . and our backfield has not got to going yet as a result."

1924

That backfield, all seniors, consisted of Jim Crowley, Elmer Layden, Don Miller, and Harry Stuhldreher. The Notre Dame Irish led at halftime, 6–0, Layden having rushed for a 10-yard touchdown.

During halftime, George Strickler, a Notre Dame student press assistant, chatted with Grantland Rice, a sportswriter with the *New York Herald-Tribune*. Rice had earlier given Grange the nickname "Galloping Ghost." Strickler described to Rice a film he had just seen, *The Four Horsemen of the Apocalypse*. Strickler was especially moved by a scene depicting the charging ghostly images of Famine, Pestilence, Destruction, and Death—the Four Horsemen. Rice had his lead for his story on Notre Dame's 13–7 win—the most famous words in sportswriting history:

"Outlined against a blue-gray October sky, the Four Horsemen rode again. In dramatic lore they are known as Famine, Pestilence, Destruction, and Death. These are only aliases. Their real names are: Stuhldreher, Miller, Crowley, and Layden."

Later that week Strickler posed the four players atop horses. Each player wore his helmet and clutched a football. Within days the photo was splashed on newspapers nationwide, and the "Four Horsemen" were born.

Rice, perhaps the most famous sportswriter during this golden age of sports, had clearly exaggerated the effectiveness of these players—and just as clearly fashioned a legend.

Rockne guided Notre Dame to a New Year's Day Rose Bowl victory over Stanford University and its first national championship. But before doing so, he taught the Four Horsemen a lesson in humility. Fearing that his four seniors had become too taken with their sudden fame, Rockne had them play on the same squad as the third-string linemen. After one particularly demoralizing series, the four backs came to the sidelines bruised and battered. Rockne asked, "Why don't you show [your opponent] your press clippings?"

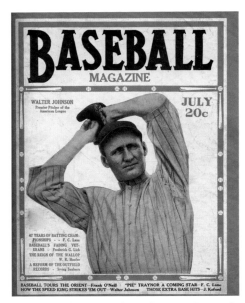

Finally a champ *This July 1924 issue of* Baseball Magazine *got it right, featuring eventual World Series hero Walter Johnson of the Washington Senators.*

Rogers Hornsby Hits .424

While Grantland Rice was crafting a legend, Rogers Hornsby was securing his. The St. Louis Cardinals second baseman won his fifth consecutive

Other Milestones of 1924

✔ The NHL awarded its first American franchise to the Boston Bruins and created the Hart Memorial Trophy to honor the league's MVP. Frank Nighbor of the Ottawa Senators was the trophy's first recipient.

✔ The Olympics added a winter version in 1924, held in Chamonix, France. American speed skater Charles Jewtraw became the first person to win a medal at what was then known as International Winter Sports Week. Jewtraw skated to victory in the 500-meter sprint.

✔ At the summer Olympics in Paris, Johnny Weissmuller won three gold medals in swimming and a bronze medal as a member of the United States water polo team. Weissmuller set Olympic records in his individual swims and also helped win a relay-team gold.

N.L. batting title, hitting .424. Hornsby's batting average was the highest single-season mark of the century. However, his league's Most Valuable Player was pitcher Dazzy Vance of the Brooklyn Dodgers.

Two years after entering the Major Leagues as a 31-year-old rookie, Vance led the N.L. in wins, earned run average, and strikeouts (262).

Washington Senators Win World Series

In the World Series, the New York Giants represented the N.L. for the fourth consecutive season, while the Washington Senators, perennial also-rans, represented the A.L.

"First in peace, first in war, and last in the American League" was the standard joke about the team from the nation's capital. That is, until second baseman Bucky Harris, just 27, became the Senators' manager in 1924. Harris had more than youth on his side—he had pitcher Walter Johnson.

"The Big Train," as Johnson was called, was in his 18th season with Washington, and it had been a dazzling one. He had the hottest fastball of his era, and Johnson led his league in victories (23), ERA (2.72), and strikeouts (158). Like Vance, he was his league's MVP.

The World Series lived up to its nickname—the Fall Classic. Four games were decided by one run, and two went into extra innings. In the seventh game, played on October 10 in the nation's capital, the Giants and Senators went into extra innings. Johnson, pitching on one day's rest, was brought in for the ninth inning. He pitched four scoreless innings and the Senators came to bat in the bottom of the 12th with the score tied, 3–3.

With one out and no one on base, Senator third baseman Muddy Ruel doubled. Two batters later, he scored, giving Washington its only World Series win in team history.

1925

Beginning of a Streak

On May 6 New York Yankees manager Miller Huggins ended shortstop Everett Scott's record for the most consecutive games played (1,307) when he replaced Scott in the lineup with Pee Wee Wanninger. Scott, whose streak had started in 1918 when he was a teammate of Babe Ruth's on the Boston Red Sox, had not missed a game in seven years.

Twenty-four days after benching Scott, Huggins sent in a 21-year-old rookie named Lou Gehrig (1903–1941) to pinch-hit for Wanninger in the eighth inning of a game. Gehrig, a big first baseman who was born and raised just a few miles from Yankee Stadium, hit a single.

Huggins was impressed. He started Gehrig at first base in place of Wally Pipp the next day. And the next. And the next one after that. Gehrig remained in the lineup for the next 14 years—an unbroken string of 2,130 games. It is a record that once seemed invincible—until Baltimore Orioles shortstop Cal Ripken, Jr., broke it in 1995.

As the story goes, Pipp, who led the American League in home runs in 1916 and 1917, complained of a headache on the date—June 1—he was benched. Pipp never regained his spot in the lineup, and later he said, "I took the two most expensive aspirins in history."

Pipp really did say that, but the truth is that it had been a poor spring for the Yankees. On April 5, Babe Ruth collapsed in a train station. He was diagnosed with an ulcer. Ruth's playboy lifestyle was at last affecting his play. This was one of only two seasons between 1918 and 1931 when he failed to lead the league in home runs. Worse, on August 9, for the only time in his record-setting career, he was taken out for a pinch hitter. The hitter, Bobby Veach, flied out.

Ruth did not return to the lineup until late May, and by then many Yankees were slumping at the plate. Pipp, the Yanks' first baseman for the previous 10 seasons, was among them. Gehrig hit .295 in Pipp's place—the last year he hit below .300 until 1939.

Red Grange Turns Pro

The Roaring Twenties had reached their midpoint, and the decade was at its peak. Although alcohol was banned nationwide, bootleggers (illegal breweries

Pro Football Hero   *The NFL was a second-class citizen to the more popular college game, until former Illinois star Red Grange joined the Chicago Bears.*

and smugglers) were producing liquor faster than G-men (government agents) could confiscate it. If anyone still wondered if athletes were national celebrities, they needed look no farther than the October 6 cover of *Time* magazine, which featured college senior and football star Harold "Red" Grange.

Seven weeks later, on October 31, Grange and Illinois traveled to Philadelphia to play Ivy League powerhouse University of Pennsylvania. Franklin Field was a sea of mud after a week of heavy rain, but Grange ran 56 yards for a touchdown on the first play from scrimmage.

The game had been greatly anticipated, because most Eastern sportswriters had never seen Grange play in person. The *New York World* sent Laurence Stallings, a famous World War I correspondent, to cover the contest. After witnessing Grange handle the ball 36 times and gain an astounding 363 yards in a 24–2 upset of Penn, Stallings said, "This story's too big for me. I can't write it."

The following day, Thanksgiving, the story got bigger. Chicago promoter C.C. Pyle (folks joked that the C.C. stood for "Cash and Carry") announced that Grange would play for the Chicago Bears in the final two games of the NFL season, then embark on a 10-game, 17-day barnstorming tour with the team.

As it turned out, Grange and the Bears played eight games in 12 grueling days. The barnstorming Bears drew crowds of 65,000 at the Polo Grounds in New York and 75,000 at the Los Angeles Coliseum. That was more than the total number of people who attended NFL games in the entire 1925 season.

Grange was sports' biggest phenomenon since Babe Ruth. He earned $80,000 for the tour. Endorsements, such as a $10,000 deal with a doll manufacturer and a $5,000 shoe deal, brought his total to more than $100,000.

It is difficult, all these years later, to put Grange's earnings—at a time when he should have been finishing his senior year in college—in perspective. But this may help: Grange earned roughly $100,000 for his first two months in the NFL. Earlier in 1925, Tim Mara spent $500 (1/200th of Grange's earnings) to buy a new NFL franchise, the New York Giants.

George Halas, the father of the NFL, later said that no player has had a greater impact on the game of football, college or professional, than Red Grange.

Vezina Succumbs to Tuberculosis

On November 28 hockey's Montreal Canadiens were hosting the Pittsburgh Penguins at the Mt. Royal Arena. Near the end of the first period, Canadien goaltender Georges Vezina began bleeding from the mouth. During the first intermission Vezina collapsed in the locker room.

Vezina, who had appeared in goal for the Canadiens in 325 consecutive games, skated onto the ice for the second period but again collapsed. He was taken off the ice and only then did his family and friends learn of his fatal condition: Vezina had tuberculosis.

Four months later, Vezina was dead at the age of 39. The first goalie in NHL history to record a shutout, Vezina led

Other Milestones of 1925

✔ On New Year's Day Notre Dame beat Stanford University in the Rose Bowl, 27–10. The Irish won, but Stanford's Ernie Nevers garnered most of the accolades after running for 114 yards, punting for a 42-yard average and making, by one estimate, three-fourths of his team's tackles—all with two broken ankles.

✔ Rogers Hornsby once more made the remarkable seem ordinary. The St. Louis Cardinals' second baseman and manager hit for his second National League Triple Crown in four seasons: He led the league in home runs (39), RBI (143), and batting average (.403). No other National Leaguer has two career Triple Crowns.

✔ On May 30 Peter DePaolo won the Indianapolis 500 and became the first race car driver to average more than 100 mph while doing so. Behind the

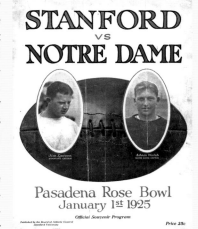

STANFORD
VS
NOTRE DAME

Pasadena Rose Bowl
January 1st 1925
Official Souvenir Program

Price 25c

1925 Rose Bowl

wheel of his Duesenberg Special, DePaolo averaged 101.13 mph.

✔ In tennis, at the U.S. Open, Bill Tilden won his sixth consecutive singles title, while Helen Wills won her third consecutive U.S. Open title. Tilden defeated his partner in Davis Cup play, Bill Johnston, for the fourth straight year.

✔ United States Patent No. 1,559,390 was issued to Fred Waller. His invention? Water skis.

✔ The University of California's Golden Bears lost for the first time since 1919, snapping a 50-game unbeaten streak. On October 10, the Olympic Athletic Club defeated the Golden Bears 15–0, ending the third-longest streak in college football history. During the streak the Golden Bears, coached by Andrew Smith, defeated opponents by an average score of 33–3.

the league in goals-against average (the average number of goals a goalie gives up per game) in 1918, 1924, and 1925. He was a crucial figure in helping the Canadiens win their first NHL Stanley Cup in 1924, but Vezina's best season was yet to come.

In 1924–25, his final full season in goal, Vezina recorded personal bests in goals-against average (1.81) and shutouts (5)—and all of this at age 38.

In the year after Vezina's death, the owners of the Canadiens donated a trophy to the league in his memory. The NHL originally awarded it annually to the goaltender on the team against which the least number of goals was scored.

Today the Vezina Trophy is given to the league's most valuable goalie, as determined by a vote of hockey broadcasters and writers.

1926

An Incredible Swim

Long before channel surfing, there was Channel swimming. Specifically, the English Channel, that 21-mile stretch of sea that separates France from Great Britain. Before 1926, only five people had successfully swum the expanse. None were Americans, and all were men.

Then came Gertrude "Trudy" Ederle of New York City. The previous August, Ederle, then 18, failed in her first attempt. She spent nearly nine hours in the water, swimming 23 miles, but a strong tide pulled her off course and she was eventually helped into her support boat.

In 1926, just after 7 a.m. on August 6, Ederle waded into the water on the French coast. The *Daily News* of London ran an editorial that read, in part: "Even the most uncompromising champion of the rights and capacities of women must admit that in contests of physical skill, speed, and endurance, they must forever remain the weaker sex."

While Britons were reading this, Ederle was swimming at 28 strokes per minute toward their shore. The water provided a favorable current. Finally, shortly after 9 p.m., Ederle waded ashore.

Only 19 years old, she had become the first woman and the first American to swim the English Channel. Ederle's time of 14 hours, 31 minutes also broke the previous record by nearly two hours.

When she returned to New York, an estimated 2 million people assembled for a ticker-tape parade in her honor. Ederle did pay a dear price for her fabulous feat, though. The frigid waters of the English Channel caused her to go deaf.

Match of the Century

Suzanne Lenglen was the first diva of women's tennis. Long before Anna Kournikova or the Williams sisters, Lenglen, of France, wore tennis outfits that revealed bare ankles and arms. Her hair was wrapped in a colorful scarf. Lenglen could also play tennis wonderfully well. By 1926 she had won six Wimbledon singles titles as well as the first two French Opens. If Lenglen was the reigning queen of tennis, Californian Helen Wills, 20, was the heiress to the throne. Six years younger, Wills had already won two U.S. Open singles titles.

The two had never met in a Grand Slam final, though (and never would). So

Splish Splash *Gertrude Ederle made history by navigating the cold, choppy waters of the English Channel.*

an exhibition event, dubbed "The Match of the Century," was arranged for them in Cannes, France, in February. The match attracted worldwide attention. Lenglen won with difficulty, 6–3, 8–6.

Wills developed appendicitis following the match, but rebounded later in the year to win her third U.S. Open in a row. Lenglen, at the request of promoter C.C. Pyle, turned pro (she and Wills were both amateurs prior to that) and toured the United States, where she earned $50,000 feasting on inferior competition. She returned to Europe a few months later and won her final Grand Slam event, the French Open.

Hagen vs. Jones

On March 7 the best professional golfer, Walter Hagen, met the best amateur, Bobby Jones, in a two-day 72-hole match play meeting.

"Everybody was saying Jones was the greatest in the world and I was second," recalled Hagen. "It rankled me a bit, so I got a friend to arrange the match—36 holes at Bob's course at Sarasota [Florida] and 36 at mine at St. Petersburg."

Hagen easily disposed of Jones, pulling 12 holes ahead with 11 to play. "It was my greatest thrill in golf." Jones bounced back to win the U.S. and British Opens.

1926

Dempsey Loses Heavyweight Title

Three years had passed since Jack Dempsey last stepped into a boxing ring for anything more than an exhibition fight. A falling out with his manager resulted in a series of legal problems that kept him out of the ring.

At last, on September 23 at Philadelphia's Sesquicentennial Field, the champ was ready to defend his title. The challenger? Gene Tunney, the "Fighting Marine," an intelligent student of tactical boxing whose gym bag contained boxing gloves and a book of poetry. An unabashed Shakespeare fan ("I worship at his shrine," Tunney said), he was the erudite opposite of the Manassa Mauler.

The largest crowd ever assembled for a championship fight (120,757 spectators paying $1,895,733) gathered under a steady rain. The champ charged from his corner at the opening bell, but Tunney, a skilled boxer, evaded him. Not only that, Tunney's counterpunches hurt the champ.

Near the end of round one, in a flurry of jabs, Tunney caught Dempsey with a right to the mouth. The champ's jaw went slack. Dempsey was hurt.

Tunney's only troublesome round was the fourth. A violent left hook caught the challenger in the throat and he stumbled forward to the ropes for support. The Dempsey who clobbered Luis Firpo in 1923 (see page 25) would have quickly finished off the challenger. But this was not the same champion. Dempsey did not throw another punch.

Tunney survived the round. The rest of the bout was downhill. The Shakespeare-quoting challenger won by unanimous decision. Dempsey, asked afterward by his wife what had happened, could only good-naturedly grimace, "I guess I forgot to duck."

Tennis Diva *This statue of Suzanne Lenglen stands outside Roland Garros Tennis Stadium near Paris (see page 38).*

Alexander Fans Lazzeri

Grover Cleveland Alexander, age 39, had nothing left to prove when he walked toward the mound on October 10 in the seventh inning of the seventh game of the World Series. The St. Louis Cardinals pitcher won a rookie-record 28 games in 1911, remains the only pitcher with three 30-win seasons, and had already won more than 300 games. He had also already beaten the Cards' foe in this Se-

Other Milestones of 1926

✔ The American Basketball League, the first professional men's league, was in its second season and insisted that the New York Original Celtics be broken up in order to make the league more competitive. After years of barnstorming together, the team's record was a stunning 1,320 wins and only 66 losses.

✔ On May 12, 38-year-old pitcher Walter Johnson beat the St. Louis Browns, 7–4, to earn his 400th career win. Only one pitcher, Cy Young, won more Major League baseball games than the "Big Train," who retired in 1927 with 417 victories.

✔ In August, former Stanford University football star Ernie Nevers showed his two-sport skills. As a rookie pitcher for the St. Louis Browns, he pitched two complete-game victories. Nevers retired from baseball in 1929 with six wins in three seasons.

---

ries, the New York Yankees, in games two and six.

Cardinals manager Rogers Hornsby was in a jam, though. St. Louis was clinging to a 3–2 lead with two outs in the seventh. The Yanks loaded the bases and hard-hitting rookie second baseman Tony Lazzeri was up. Alexander, meanwhile, was asleep in the bullpen. Legend has it that he was hung over after a night of drinking when Hornsby summoned him to pitch, although other reports dispute that claim. Regardless, here was a 39-year old pitcher approaching the mound who had just pitched a complete game the day before.

"Alex, we're in a tough spot," said Hornsby, handing his pitcher the ball. "There's no place to put Lazzeri."

"I reckon I better strike him out," Alexander replied.

In one of the classic confrontations in World Series history, Alexander struck out Lazzeri on four pitches.

Alexander then retired the next five batters. With two outs in the ninth inning, Babe Ruth came to bat. Ruth had homered three times in one game earlier in the series—the first person to do that. Wisely, Alexander walked Ruth.

With Lou Gehrig at bat, Ruth attempted to steal second base. Cardinals catcher Bob O'Farrell, the National League MVP, threw him out easily. St. Louis had its first World Series championship.

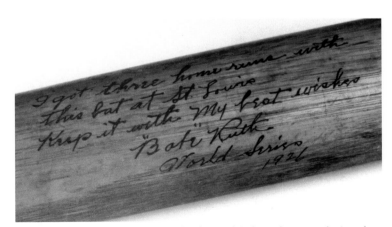

Babe's Bat *Babe Ruth used this bat to hit three homers during the 1926 World Series. His homers were not enough, though, and the Babe ended up as the "goat" of the Series, making the final out.*

1927

The Harlem Globetrotters

Abe Saperstein stepped into his Model-T Ford on the crisp, clear Chicago afternoon of January 7. Accompanying Saperstein—a portly, short, 24-year-old white man—were five African-American men, all of them much taller than he. They were outfitted in red, white, and blue striped uniforms that read "NEW YORK," stitched together in Saperstein's father's tailor shop. Their destination: Hinckley, Illinois, 48 miles away.

The Harlem Globetrotters were beginning their first road trip.

Saperstein was born in London, but his birth date (July 4, 1901) showed him to be a man destined for America. As a student at the University of Illinois, he begged to try out for the basketball team. The coach took one look at Saperstein, who was just five feet tall, and refused.

Now, here Saperstein was, coach and general manager of his own basketball team. He had originally called the team the Savoy Big Five, after a Chicago ballroom where they played their games. But he soon changed the name to the Harlem Globetrotters, even though none of the original five Globetrotters—Walter "Toots" Wright, Byron "Fats" Long, Willis "Kid" Oliver, Andy Washington, and Al "Runt" Pullins—had ever seen New York, much less Harlem.

For their first game in Hinckley, the Globetrotters drew 300 people and earned $75. Saperstein, who had bought the Model-T from a funeral home, was happy to have made back his gasoline money.

After that, Saperstein booked games wherever he could. The Model-T drove through the rural Midwest, bringing basketball to folks who had mostly never seen it and almost certainly had never seen an all-black team. They eked out a meager living and rarely ever lost. Over the winter the Globetrotters' record was 101–16.

Their nickname ("Clown Princes of Basketball"), their theme song ("Sweet Georgia Brown," which had been a hit in 1926), their crowd-pleasing showmanship—all of that came later. In 1927, they were simply a team that hoped to live up to the name they had given themselves.

"We chose Harlem because, well, because Harlem was to the fellows what Jerusalem is to us," said Saperstein, who was Jewish. "And Globetrotters? Well, we

Murderers' Row   *Lou Gehrig, Bob Meusel, Tony Lazzeri, and Babe Ruth made up a fearsome quartet of hitters. The inset photo shows a press pin given to reporters covering the 1927 World Series.*

had dreams. We hoped to travel. We made it, all right. We made it all the way to Israel, as a matter of fact." By 2002, the Globetrotters had played and entertained in more than 115 countries.

Murderers' Row

It's one of those unanswerable debates that baseball fans love so much, but according to many experts there might never have been a better baseball team than the 1927 New York Yankees. This particular edition of the Bronx Bombers, the heart of whose lineup was known as "Murderers' Row," went 110–44 and won the American League pennant by 19 games. To climax their historic season, the Yankees swept the Pittsburgh Pirates, 4–0, in the World Series.

Certainly, teams have won more regular-season games. The 1906 Chicago Cubs and the 2001 Seattle Mariners both

1927

won 116. Neither of those teams won the World Series, though. The 1998 Yankees won 114 games and, like their pinstriped predecessors, swept the Series. Still, there was something so dominant about the 1927 Yankees that even now it is just about impossible to rank any other team above them.

Start with Babe Ruth, who, batting third in the lineup, broke his own home

run record by one, blasting 60 homers—the first man to reach that total (his record stood until Roger Maris hit 61 in 1961). Batting fourth was Lou Gehrig, who hit 47 home runs, the most any player not named Ruth had ever whacked in one season. Gehrig also had a record-setting 175 RBI. Who knows how many more RBI Gehrig might have had if Ruth hadn't homered so often right before him in the lineup? Then again, Gehrig single-handedly prevented Ruth from achieving the Triple Crown, since he was the only player in the American League who had more RBI (Ruth had 164) and a higher batting average than the Babe.

Four players drove in more than 100 runs. The team batting average was .307. Gehrig batted .378. Ruth and Earle Combs hit .356. Tony Lazzeri hit .309, and his 18 homers were third-best in the league behind Ruth and Gehrig. All four would one day enter the Baseball Hall of Fame. The team slugging percentage—.498—is an all-time record.

The numbers are numbing, but how better to display this lineup's outrageous power? Well, legend has it that the Pirates were so intimidated watching the Yankees take batting practice before game one of the World Series that playing the games was merely a formality.

Hagen Wins Fourth Straight PGA Title

Walter Hagen was on a fishing trip in Wisconsin when conscience got the better of him. Although he had not touched a golf club in weeks, the man who had won the last three PGA Champion-

Champion Golfer *Walter Hagen (left), shown here with an unidentified caddie, had a spectacular year in golf, winning his fourth PGA Championship and helping the U.S. win the Ryder Cup.*

ships decided, at the last minute, to defend his title.

Hagen said later, "Well, I just got to thinking that if I didn't play, much of the credit would be taken away from the man who won. People would say, 'It would have been different if Hagen had played.'"

Had he asked the other golfers, they probably would have told Hagen, "Don't do us any favors."

Hagen, the premier pro golfer of the era, was renowned for both his self-confidence and, of course, his talent. In 1924, needing a six-foot putt to win the British Open in rainy conditions, Hagen tapped the ball and, as it still rolled, turned and tossed his putter to the caddy. The crowd's roar confirmed what Hagen knew to be a foregone conclusion.

In June in Dallas, Texas, at the PGA Championship, Hagen, 34, showed signs of rust but not enough for anyone else in the field to catch him. The Rochester, New York, native captured his fourth straight PGA title, becoming not only the first but also the last man to win the same Major tournament four years in a row. No one has yet duplicated his feat.

"I didn't think I had one chance in a million to win for the fourth consecutive time," Hagen said. He was wrong.

U.S. Wins the First Ryder Cup

The PGA Championship was the perfect ending to a brilliant year for Hagen. Earlier in June, Hagen captained the inaugural United States Ryder Cup team. The Yanks defeated their opponents from Great Britain, 9 1/2 to 2 1/2.

Informal matches between golfers from the two nations had led businessman Samuel Ryder to donate a gold trophy and work to set up a match to be played every other year between top golfers from each side of the Atlantic. Hagen led the U.S. team, while former British Open champ Ted Ray was captain of the British squad.

The event was played at the Worcester (Massachusetts) Country Club from June 3–5. The date was chosen so British players could make the six-day ocean crossing for the Ryder Cup, then stay for the U.S. Open two weeks later.

Future Masters champion Gene Sarazen and Hagen helped win matches on the first day, and the Americans never looked back. Bedeviled by poor putting, the British team was roundly defeated. Two years later in England, though, they got revenge.

America and Great Britain split the first four Ryder Cups, then America won 17 of 18 events from 1935 to 1977. The tournament format switched to a U.S. team versus an all-European team in 1979, and it remains one of the premier events in the sport.

Dempsey-Tunney Rematch: The Long Count

The September 22 heavyweight championship fight between Jack Dempsey and Gene Tunney contained the longest five seconds—and one of the most famous moments—in boxing history.

"The Long Count," as it came to be called, happened in the seventh round of the much-anticipated rematch between

1927 the two heavyweights. They fought in front of 104,943 spectators in Chicago's Soldier Field. The gate was $2.65 million, a record for a single fight that would last 50 years.

As in their first meeting (see page 40), Tunney was the technically superior boxer, the matador toying with Dempsey the bull. But then, less than a minute into round seven, Dempsey's right-left-right combination sent Tunney sprawling toward the ropes.

As Tunney was falling, Dempsey landed a four-punch combination that set the fans in the stadium screaming.

Stand in the Corner *Jack Dempsey just couldn't back off when he knocked down Gene Tunney in their famous rematch. It gave Tunney crucial extra seconds of rest in the bout.*

Another 50 million boxing fans, listening to announcer Graham McNamee's radio broadcast from ringside, were also whipped into a frenzy.

Dave Barry, the referee, motioned Dempsey to a neutral corner. The Manassa Mauler, who had knocked Luis Firpo down seven times in one round four years earlier simply by hitting Firpo as soon as he got to one knee (see page 25), replied, "I'll stay here."

Dempsey was standing in his own corner. Barry approached him and half pushed him to the proper corner. Then the referee returned to the fallen champ. Instead of picking up the timekeeper's count at six (which had begun when Tunney hit the canvas), Barry began again at one.

Tunney stayed down until Barry said, "nine." Tunney had been on the canvas at least 14 seconds, but he later insisted that he could have risen earlier. His corner motioned for him to remain down and get extra rest.

Tunney survived the round, and for the final three rounds prudently avoided Dempsey. Tunney, a former Marine, won by a unanimous decision. Afterward, Dempsey was asked why he had not retreated to a neutral corner. The Illinois Boxing Commission rulebook was clear:

> When a knockdown occurs, the timekeeper shall immediately arise and announce the seconds audibly as they elapse. The referee shall first see that the opponent retires to the farthest corner, and then, turning to the timekeeper, shall pick up the count in unison with the timekeeper, announcing the seconds to the boxer on

Other Milestones of 1927

✔ Helen Wills, recovered from appendicitis, won the first of four straight Wimbledon tennis singles finals. The Phi Beta Kappa from the University of California began a winning streak of 158 consecutive matches without surrendering even a set.

✔ On July 18 Ty Cobb, now with the Philadelphia Athletics, doubled off Sam Gibson of the Detroit Tigers for the 4,000th hit of his career. He became the first baseball player to reach the 4,000–hit plateau.

✔ The NFL shrunk from 22 teams to 12. The New York Giants allowed just 20 points to be scored against them all season and were crowned champions.

✔ Notre Dame, the Fighting Irish, wore green jerseys for the first time in a football game versus Army, discarding the blue jerseys that had been a tradition since 1887. Army handed Notre Dame its only loss of the season, 18–0. The school has continued the green jerseys to this day, bringing them out for big games (right)

Notre Dame in green

the floor. Should the boxer on his feet fail to stay in the corner, the referee and timekeeper shall cease counting until he has so retired.

Dempsey, in the manner that made him so beloved to millions of fight fans, made no excuses. "I couldn't move," he said. "I just couldn't. I wanted Tunney to get up. I wanted to kill the [guy]."

The fight, which took place eight days before Babe Ruth hit his record-breaking 60th home run, was the sports event of the year. Promoter Tex Rickard paid Dempsey $425,000 for his efforts and Tunney, who would fight only once more before retiring, $990,000. How grand a payday was that? Ruth, the biggest sports star of his era, earned $80,000 the same year.

1928

Sore Feet

The 1920s seemed to breed odd events, most of which were marathons of one sort or another. Flagpole-sitting, dancing, talking—people wanted to see who could do what for the longest time. One promoter named C.C. Pyle had perhaps the ultimate marathon idea—a 2,800-mile footrace from Los Angeles to New York, the Transcontinental Race. First prize would be $25,000.

On March 4 at Los Angeles's Ascot Speedway, 199 runners lined up as football hero Red Grange gave the starting signal. After the first 16-mile leg, from Los Angeles to Puente, California, 76 of the racers dropped out.

Pyle's Transcontinental Race became a laughingstock. A skeptical press dubbed it the Bunion Derby. People joked that C.C. no longer stood for "Cash and Carry," but rather "Corn and Callus."

By the time the "aching dog caravan" arrived at Madison Square Garden in New York 84 days later, an arena of mostly empty seats was on hand to greet the 19-year-old winner, Andrew Payne. The victor accepted his prize, then stumbled into a concrete pillar and fell unconscious.

A Coach in the Net

The tale of Lester Patrick's night in goal is one of the wildest in hockey history. The New York Rangers had only been in the National Hockey League two seasons when they traveled north to Canada to face the Montreal Maroons in the Stanley Cup finals. The odds were heavily against the Rangers and their 44-year-old coach, Patrick. No team based in the United States had won the Cup in the league's 10 years, and, due to a scheduling conflict that had a circus occupying Madison Square Garden, the Rangers' home ice, the best-of-five series was played entirely at the Montreal Forum.

On April 14, the odds got a lot worse. The Rangers had already lost the first game. Now, in the second period of game two with the score tied 0–0, Nels Stewart of the Maroons bore down on Rangers goalie Lorne Chabot. Stewart, who had one of the hardest slapshots in the league, sent a missile that smacked into Chabot's forehead before the goalie had time to react. He crumpled to the ice, unconscious and bleeding profusely.

As Chabot was carted off to the hospital (he did recover), Patrick conferred with Maroons coach Eddie Gerard. In those days, teams had fewer players. It was not uncommon to borrow a player for an evening. "I'd like permission to use Alex Connell of the Ottawa Senators," said Patrick, mentioning another NHL player. "He's in the rink [as a spectator] and I'm sure he'd play for us."

"No," Gerard replied. "You can't use Connell!"

Patrick was furious. The Rangers had no goalie. The Maroons, meanwhile, had Clint Benedict in goal. Benedict had the lowest goals-against average in six of the NHL's previous 10 seasons.

James Burchard, who covered hockey for the *New York World-Telegram*, happened to be in the Rangers' locker room. "Go on, Lester," said Burchard. "Show 'em what you're made of." Patrick had played in the NHL, true, but he had retired seven years earlier. Besides, he was a defenseman, not a goalie.

"Okay," said Patrick, "I'll do it."

What followed was one of the most miraculous performances in the history of sport. For the next two periods plus an overtime, Patrick was nearly flawless. He stopped 18 of 19 shots, and the scored was tied 1–1 after regulation time.

The game went into sudden-death overtime. Frank Boucher of the Rangers sent a shot past Benedict. The Rangers won, 2–1. The stunned Forum crowd could only watch in silence as the Rangers lifted their coach—now also their goalie—into the air and carried him off the ice.

The Rangers won two more on the Maroons' home ice and thus the title. The Stanley Cup came to the United States for the first time.

Tragic Hero *Notre Dame football star George Gipp's death at age 25 spurred a legendary request (see page 50).*

1928

To the Winners *The players on the 1928 New York Yankees each got a silver watch for winning the World Series.*

Yankees Sweep Again

Poor Lou Gehrig! The Yankees' first baseman always seemed to follow teammate Babe Ruth, whether in the batting order or in overall greatness.

The New York Yankees returned to the World Series in October for the third straight year. Their opponent was the St. Louis Cardinals, the team that had beaten them two years earlier. All Gehrig did as the Yankees swept the Cards 4–0 was bat .545, hit four home runs, and drive in a World Series-record nine runs (one-third of the Yankees' total).

Only Ruth could outshine Gehrig, and he did. The Babe hit .625, a World Series record. In the series-clinching fourth game at Sportsman's Park in St. Louis, Ruth hit three home runs. It was a feat only Ruth had accomplished before, in 1926—also in game four of the Series at Sportsman's Park against the Cardinals.

On the second of Ruth's three home runs, the Babe struck out—sort of. The St.

Louis pitcher threw a quick strike that fooled Ruth, who was not ready for the delivery and swung. The umpire disallowed the pitch and, Ruth, given an extra swing, hammered the next pitch into the right field pavilion.

"Win One for the Gipper"

Notre Dame football coach Knute Rockne suffered through the worst season of his 13-year career but produced his most glorious and memorable moment. Four of Rockne's 12 losses in his 13 seasons in South Bend, Indiana, came in 1928. Had it not been for the godfather of all halftime speeches, Notre Dame might have lost five games this season and, in so doing, handed Rockne the only losing season of his career.

The Fighting Irish of Notre Dame entered Yankee Stadium on November 10 a shadow of the team that had gone 34–4–2 the past four seasons. Already, the Irish had lost at University of Wisconsin and Georgia Tech. This afternoon's opponent, Army, had defeated the Irish 18–0 last autumn. The Army, a team also known as the Cadets, had won six straight, and included many of the college football stars of that day, including All-American halfback Chris Cagle.

The teams played to a scoreless tie in the first half. Notre Dame squandered a scoring chance when Fred Collins fumbled the ball into the end zone, and it was recovered by a Cadet. Inside the locker room, Rockne, cigar in hand, stared at the ceiling. He spoke as if he were delivering a eulogy. The coach told his team about how, eight years earlier, he went to visit

Other Milestones of 1928

A trio of important sports figures ended their careers this year.

✔ Heavyweight champion Gene Tunney knocked out challenger Tom Heeney in July and earned $525,000 for the effort. He promptly retired. Tunney did not need the money. Later this year, he married an heiress to the Andrew Carnegie fortune. (Carnegie was a Scottish immigrant who made a fortune in the steel business. He was one of the richest men in the world.)

✔ Johnny Weissmuller, who won three individual and two relay Olympic gold medals in swimming, traded in his

Ty Cobb

swimsuit for a loincloth. Weissmuller, who in the next decade portrayed Tarzan in numerous films, left the pool having set 67 world records at every distance from 100 meters to 800 meters.

✔ Ty Cobb, the greatest offensive player in Major League Baseball history, finally hung up his high-flying spikes after 24 seasons. "The Georgia Peach" retired with a lifetime record of 4,191 hits, 892 stolen bases and a .367 batting average. Nearly 50 years passed before any of those records were broken. The batting average mark still stands.

---

the great George Gipp on his deathbed. Gipp had been a Notre Dame All-American who died at the age of 25 of an infection (see page 13). "Remember that name," Rockne told them. "Never forget it."

Then Rockne shared with his team the last words Gipp said to him—at least according to Rockne. "Someday, Rock," Gipp said, "when things on the field are going against us, tell the boys, Rock, to go out and win just one for the Gipper. Now, I don't know where I'll be then, Coach. But I'll know about it, and I'll be happy."

Rockne waited a few moments for the words to sink in. Players were crying. "Boys," said Rockne, "I'm convinced that this is the game George Gipp would want us to win. Okay, let's go and get 'em."

The Irish did just that. Army scored first in the second half, but Notre Dame responded with a touchdown to tie the score, 6–6.

With the score still tied late in the fourth quarter, Rockne sent in little-used 6-foot-3 receiver Johnny O'Brien. A long pass came his way. O'Brien, stumbling, caught the ball at the 10-yard line, juggled it and dove into the end zone as a pair of Cadets hit him. The result: Notre Dame 12, Army 6.

Since that game, the phrase "Win one for the Gipper" has become part of the American lexicon. It is used to inspire everyone from athletes to businessmen. Former actor Ronald Reagan, who played Gipp in a movie (*Knute Rockne: All-American*) and was elected to two terms as president, enjoyed connecting his electoral victories to the spirit of the former Notre Dame star.

1929

"Wrong Way" Riegels

Roy Riegels might have thought, as he rumbled toward the end zone, that he was heading into sports immortality. He was . . . just not the way he thought he would be famous.

Tennis Ace *Helen Wills, later Helen Wills Moody, was one of the dominant athletes of the era.*

Riegels was the center for the University of California, which was playing Georgia Tech in the Rose Bowl game. In the second quarter, with the score tied 0–0, Tech's Stumpy Thomason fumbled. Riegels scooped up the ball near the 30-yard line and started one of the most infamous plays in college football history. "I was running toward the sidelines," he said the next day, "and when I picked up the ball I started to turn to my left toward Tech's goal. Somebody shoved me and I bounded right off into a tough tackler. In pivoting to get away from him, I completely lost my bearings."

Riegels ran full-speed toward his team's own end zone. Teammate Benny Lom chased after Riegels the entire way, yelling, "No, Roy! No! Not that way!"

Riegels never heard Lom. He slowed down as he neared the goal line. Lom caught Riegels and turned him around, whereupon he was crushed by a wave of Tech tacklers on the one-yard line.

On the ensuing play, California decided to punt. Lom's punt was blocked out of the end zone for a safety. Tech went on to win 8–7. Riegels wanted to stay out of the second half, but coach Clarence "Nibs" Price waited a few minutes, then said, "Roy, get up and go back," Price replied. "The game is only half over." Riegels played well in the second half, but the damage was done—to the score and to his place in sports history.

Wills Wins . . . Again

Helen Wills dominated tennis. She did not lose a single set she played from 1927 to 1933. In 1929, she won all three Grand Slam events that she entered—the French Open, Wimbledon and the U.S. Open, matching her 1928 feat.

Wills won 19 Grand Slam singles titles during the course of her career, and never apologized for her demeanor. "I had one thought," she later said, "and that was to put the ball across the net."

Athletics Win World Series

Cornelius MacGillicuddy, better known as Connie Mack, owned and managed the Philadelphia Athletics for 50 seasons, from 1901 through 1950. Mack holds the Major League Baseball all-time managerial records for both wins (3,755) and losses (3,967). He won six World Series, but Mack never had a better team than he did in 1929.

The 1928 edition of the Athletics boasted a Hall of Fame outfield of Ty Cobb, Tris Speaker, and Al Simmons. Cobb and Speaker were at the end of long careers, however, and their retirement energized the Athletics.

Mule Haas and Bing Miller, their outfield replacements, both hit well over .300 this season. Simmons, meanwhile, batted .365 and had an American League-best

High Scorer *Ernie Nevers was one of early pro football's greatest stars. His single-game scoring record of 40 points remains an all-time best more than 70 years later (see page 54).*

1929

157 RBI. The Athletics won with pitching and defense, though, committing the fewest errors in the A.L. while leading the league with the lowest ERA. So dominant was Mack's team that it won the pennant over the New York Yankees of Babe Ruth and Lou Gehrig by 18 games.

Everyone expected the Athletics' ace, Lefty Grove, to start for Philadelphia in game one of the World Series. Instead, Mack sent his seventh-best pitcher, Howard Ehmke, to see the Cubs play in person and scout them in the last days of the season. The fans were shocked to see Ehmke take the mound. The veteran right-hander, responded with a complete-game 3–1 victory.

The teams split the next two games. In game four at Philadelphia's Shibe Park, the Cubs led 8–0 entering the bottom of the seventh inning. It appeared that the Series would soon be tied, two games all.

Then the Athletics exploded for 10 runs in the seventh inning, stunning the Cubs and winning 10–8. After blowing an eight-run lead in game four, Chicago blew a two-run lead in game five. Philadelphia and its mainstay manager had its first World Series title since 1913.

Nevers Goes for 40

Scoring 40 points in a pro basketball game is quite an achievement. Scoring 40 points in a pro football game is practically unheard of. In fact, it has only been done once.

On Thanksgiving Day, November 28, the Chicago Bears met their Windy City rivals, the Chicago Cardinals. The Cardinals' best player was Ernie Nevers, who entered the league with much fanfare in 1926. In that year, Nevers, a Minnesota native, was signed by the Duluth Eskimos. However, such was the clamor to watch the brawny (6-foot-1, 205 pounds) blond fullback play that the Eskimos became a touring squad. Officially, they changed their name to Ernie Nevers' Eskimos.

In 1926, the Eskimos played 29 games. Of the 1,740 minutes of play, it is estimated that Nevers, carrying the ball on

Baseball Men *No man led a Major League Baseball team for more years (50) than Philadelphia's Connie Mack (right), shown here meeting with New York Yankees manager Bob Shawkey.*

Other Milestones of 1929

✔ In the realm of silly sports, Alvin "Shipwreck" Kelly sat atop a flagpole above New York's Paramount Hotel for 13 days, 13 hours and 13 minutes in May. Oddly, a pamphlet Kelly had prepared about himself for onlookers below sold exactly 13 copies.

✔ At golf's U.S. Open in June, Al Espinosa took Bobby Jones to a second playoff round before finally losing. For Jones, it was his third Open win.

✔ It was a good year to be named Lefty and play in Philadelphia. Lefty Grove of baseball's Philadelphia Athletics led the American League in victories (20)

Lefty O'Doul

and E.R.A. (2.81). Lefty O'Doul of the Philadelphia Phillies won baseball's batting crown, hitting .398, and set the National League record for hits in one season (254) that still stands. O'Doul, a former Yankees' pitcher, was out of the big leagues for four seasons before returning in 1928 as an outfielder.

✔ In the NFL, the Green Bay Packers, led by the elusive running of Johnny "Blood" McNally and coach Earl "Curly" Lambeau, went 12–0–1 and were named NFL champions (the league's first championship game was played four years later, in 1933).

---

nearly every offensive down and playing defense full time, played 1,714 of those minutes. The following season, 1927, provided much of the same for Nevers, who was also a Major League Baseball pitcher and found time to serve up two of Babe Ruth's record-breaking 60 home runs.

Nevers sat out the entire 1928 season, recovering from all the injuries he'd accumulated. In the interim, the Duluth team folded, so Nevers joined the Cardinals. On Thanksgiving Day, he not only scored all of his team's points, but he also scored more points than anyone else in

the NFL, before or since, has scored in a single game.

Nevers' 40 points came on six touchdown runs and four extra-point kicks. Following the game, Chicago Bears coach George Halas said, "Final score: Bears 6, Nevers 40."

As impressive and seemingly untouchable as Nevers' record is—it remained unbroken through this book's publication—he also scored all of the Chicago Cardinals' points four days earlier in a 19–0 defeat of Dayton. In those two games, Nevers scored 59 straight points for his team.

1930

Truth or Fiction?

The 1930s were the heyday of the Negro Leagues. These were the professional baseball leagues set up by African-American owners and players because Major League clubs would not allow black players to play. Some of the finest ballplayers of all time—of any background—took part in the Negro Leagues. That they could not play in the Major League remains one of the lowlights in the history of American sports. But they played on, and they played great baseball.

One of the greatest players made his debut this year. On July 25, the Homestead Grays of the Negro National League were hosting the Kansas City Monarchs. The Grays' starting catcher was injured and the team needed a player.

Legend has it that an 18-year-old who was sitting in the stands, Josh Gibson (1911–1947), was called to step in. Gibson was a hard-hitting catcher for a local semi-pro team, the Crawford Colored Giants. Gibson left his seat and played. The Grays soon signed Gibson, who became known as the greatest hitter in Negro League history. In fact, he was commonly referred to as "the black Babe Ruth."

A less spectacular account of Gibson's debut goes like this: catcher Buck Ewing did split his finger, but in an earlier game. Cum Posey, a co-owner of the Grays, sent a taxi to fetch Gibson, who was playing across town (this was in Pittsburgh) for the Colored Giants. Gibson made it to the ballpark a few innings later and never returned to semi-pro ball.

Whichever story you want to believe, Ewing's injury launched the career of one of history's greatest hitters. Later this season, Gibson's Grays traveled to Yankee Stadium to play the New York Lincoln Giants for a Negro League championship series. In one game, Gibson hit a ball 500 feet into the left field bullpen. For years, fans claimed it was the longest home run ever hit in Yankee Stadium.

Gallant Fox

Eleven years passed before a second member joined the exclusive Triple Crown fraternity begun in 1919 by the great racehorse Sir Barton. The second three-year-old to win the Kentucky Derby, Preakness Stakes and Belmont Stakes was Gallant Fox, a big bay colt with what was known as a "wild right eye." The eye

The Best Ever? *Some observers believe Josh Gibson was the best power hitter ever.*

had too much white around the pupils, and it was said that any horse drawing up to pass Gallant Fox on the outside would glance at the eye and become too frightened to pass.

That may be a legend. Indeed, few horses had the speed to stay with Gallant Fox, much less pass him, in 1930. He won the Preakness, which was run before the Kentucky Derby, by three-quarters of a

1930

length. At Churchill Downs, he won the Derby by two lengths.

Despite those victories, Gallant Fox was not the favorite at Belmont Park for the third leg of the Triple Crown. The favored horse, Whichone, who had missed the other two races due to injury, was thought to be invincible. Instead, Gallant Fox silenced his critics, leading the race from start to finish and winning by three lengths.

After the Belmont, which was run in a light drizzle, sportswriter Charles Hatton used the phrase "Triple Crown" to describe Gallant Fox's feat, thus coining horse racing's most famous term.

Few horses have enjoyed better years than Gallant Fox did in 1930. He entered 10 races and won nine. His only loss was a second-place finish at the Travers Stakes to a 100-to-1 shot named Jim Dandy. He retired at the end of 1930 as the sport's career leader in earnings ($328,165), and even then he was not done. Five years later, his legacy was enriched when one of his offspring, Omaha, won the Triple Crown. Gallant Fox thus became the first Triple Crown winner to sire another Triple Crown winner.

Bobby Jones Wins Grand Slam

Amateur golfer Bobby Jones had already won nine Major championships when the new decade dawned. Twice he won the British Open, three times the U.S. Open and four times the United States Amateur. He had never won the British Amateur, however, the fourth and final piece of the four-tournament puzzle that George Trevor, an eminent golf writer of the time, called the Impregnable Quadrilateral of Golf.

No golfer had ever won all four events, and certainly not in the same calendar year. As 1930 dawned, British

Silver for the Slam *Golfing legend Bobby Jones holds the trophy he was awarded after winning the 1930 U.S. Open. It was one-quarter of the four-event Grand Slam he won that year.*

insurance company Lloyds of London quoted the odds as 50 to 1 against Jones capturing all four Majors this year.

Jones's first obstacle was the British Amateur at St. Andrews, Scotland, in May. This was the tournament he had never won, and had never even come close to winning. This time he did.

Two weeks later, Jones won the British Open at Royal Liverpool in Hoylake, England. Suddenly the world's greatest golfer was halfway home and the previously inconceivable idea of one man sweeping all four tournaments in one year no longer seemed so outrageous.

On the third leg of his quest, the U.S. Open at Interlachen Country Club in Minneapolis, Minnesota, Jones was the beneficiary of good fortune. On one hole, he was facing a shot over a lake and onto an island green. As Jones was on the downward part of his swing, two girls rushed from the gallery seeking his autograph. Distracted, Jones topped the ball (hit the top of the ball instead of underneath it), sending the ball forward like a line drive, rather than his planned high arc.

But the ball, instead of torpedoing into the lake, skipped across it as if it were a flat stone. It landed on the fairway, 30 yards from the green. Golf historians refer to it as the lily pad shot. Jones won the U.S. Open.

All that was left now was the U. S. Amateur. The tournament was held at Merion Golf Club outside of Philadelphia—the same course where Jones had made his championship golf debut in 1916. Before a gallery of 18,000 spectators on September 27, Jones handily defeated Gene Homans 8 and 7. (The tournament was in match play, in which golfers play to win each hole, rather than comparing their total score for the round. The final total meant Jones won eight more holes than Homans, with seven to play, thus ensuring victory.)

Needing to sink his putt on the 11th hole to stay alive, Homans hit it and made his way over to shake Jones' hand before the errant shot stopped rolling. A roar went up from the crowd. Jones had done something no other golfer had ever done: win all four Majors in one calendar year. O.B. Keeler of the *Atlanta Journal* described the feat using a term that would stick, the Grand Slam. Then, making as graceful an exit as a sport has ever seen, Jones retired at the top of his, or anyone's, game. He was 28 years old.

At year's end, the first Sullivan Award honoring the nation's outstanding amateur athlete was announced (see page 61). The recipient? Bobby Jones, who to this day remains the only man ever to capture the Grand Slam in one calendar year.

America's Cup

In 1851, a new match race between ocean-going yachts was held between boats from America and Great Britain. America won that first race, and the trophy became known as the America's Cup. Held every few years, or when a challenge is made to the Cup holder, it remains the premier international sailing race. America held the Cup from that first race in 1851 until 1983, when a team from Australia won it.

In 1930, the Americans were still the top dogs on the sea, but British tea mag-

1930

nate Harold Lipton was still trying to capture the Cup. Lipton had made four other challenges since 1899 and had lost each of those series of races.

Lipton's final attempt came on a boat named *Shamrock V* in a contest against *Enterprise* in September, skippered by American millionaire Harold Vanderbilt. *Shamrock V* was soundly defeated in four straight races in the best-of-seven series. The Cup remained firmly in American hands and Lipton went back home empty-handed. However, he was savvy enough to use his continuing presence in the American media due to the races to promote sales of his tea, which became a best-seller in America.

News for Fans *Produced by the Spalding company—founded by a former star player—this annual magazine was many fans' guide to each baseball season.*

Hack Wilson Sets RBI Record

If Lewis "Hack" Wilson were an animal, he would be a bulldog. The Chicago Cubs' outfielder had a unique physique. He stood 5-foot-6 and weighed nearly 200 pounds. Wilson had a massive, barrel chest that flowed into a tree-trunk neck (size 18) and a pair of arms that were thicker than most baseball player's legs. Imagine a fire hydrant wearing tiny size six shoes—that was Wilson.

Wilson really knew how to do two things well: hit a baseball and drink. In 1930, the free-swinging, right-handed slugger put together perhaps the greatest power-hitting season in National League history. He walloped 56 home runs, an N.L. record that was not broken until 1998, and batted .356 with an outrageous .723 slugging percentage.

Most immortal of Wilson's feats, however, were his eye-popping 190 RBI. There are records, after all, and then there are records. Since 1938, the closest anyone in either league has come to eclipsing Wilson's mark is 165 RBI.

Alas, Wilson squandered much of his talent and money with his heavy drinking. His manager, Joe McCarthy gently tried to convince his slugger to stop drinking. But Wilson died at the age of 48, penniless and virtually alone. In 1999, baseball historians discovered that a mistake had been made in a 1930 box score and that an RBI that should have been attributed to Wilson was given to someone else. Correcting the error, they gave Wilson his 191st RBI for the 1930 season, putting the record that much farther out of reach.

Other Milestones of 1930

✔ Clarence DeMar, who won his first Boston Marathon in 1911, won the last of his record seven Boston races this year on April 19 at the age of 41. DeMar, who entered 33 Boston Marathons (the last in 1954 at age 65), won in a time of 2:34:48.

✔ Helen Wills Moody won her fourth consecutive Wimbledon tennis singles final in July. On the following day, Bill Tilden won his third championship at Wimbledon and his first since 1921.

✔ In an exhibition game versus Major League Baseball players, Negro League pitcher Leroy "Satchel" Paige (1906–1982) struck out 22 batters. The Major League record for strikeouts in one game is 21, set in 1962 by Tom Cheney in a 16-inning game. The nine-inning record is 20, set by several pitchers.

Trojans on the Track

Dean Cromwell had already been the track and field coach at the University of Southern California (USC) for 21 seasons when his Trojans won the national championship in 1930. Cromwell had certainly had some great athletes even before this year. He had already coached Olympic gold medalists such as Fred Kelly (Stockholm, 1912) and Charles Paddock (Antwerp, 1920). He had even guided the Trojans to a national title, albeit an unofficial one, in 1926.

However, this was the year Cromwell's Trojans officially became a force to be reckoned with. It was a force that lasted a long time. It became one of the longest runs of success in college sports.

From 1930 until he retired in 1948, Cromwell coached USC to 11 national championships. Even more impressive, the Trojans lost only three dual meets (track meets in which only two teams participate) in those 19 seasons.

Sullivan Award Makes Its Debut

Year-end awards have become a big part of every sports season. In 1930, the nation's major award for amateur athletes was introduced.

The James E. Sullivan Award was first presented by the Amateur Athletic Union to golfer Bobby Jones (see page 58). The citation read, then as now, that the award went to the athlete who "by his [or her] performance, example and influence as an amateur, has done the most during the year to advance the cause of sportsmanship."

The Sullivan Award remains today a high honor, and some of America's greatest sporting names have received the trophy. Swimmer Ann Curtis became the first female winner in 1944.

1931

No Refueling: A Diesel-Powered Indy 500

On February 5 at Daytona Beach, Florida, Malcolm Campbell set a new world record for speed on land. Driving a 1,450-horsepower car through a wet mist and using five miles of straight-away to build up his speed, Campbell covered a mile in 14.60 seconds—he drove 246.575 miles per hour.

Campbell's record was certainly impressive—he beat the existing world record by more than 14 m.p.h.—but it has since been surpassed many times by many daring individuals in faster and faster cars. A much more unique driving record, and one that may never be repeated, was set on May 30 at the 19th running of the Indianapolis 500.

When Indiana native Clessie Cummins entered his car at Indy, he never for a moment believed he had the fastest car at the Indianapolis track fondly known as the Brickyard. But he believed he had the most durable one. "I have the sturdiest, most reliable engine," said Cummins, who hired veteran driver Dave Evans to race his vehicle, "and we'll prove it by making the distance without stopping."

Cummins had converted a diesel boat engine for his car. A diesel car had never raced in the Indy 500 before. The advantage: no pit stops to refuel, and that saves time. The disadvantage: by carrying more fuel, and highly explosive fuel at that, Cummins's car posed a big risk to its driver. Just before the start of the race, Evans said to Cummins, "Whatever you do, don't let them cremate me."

Fortunately, it never came to that. Evans completed all 500 miles of the race without a single pit stop, finishing in 13th place. It was the last time a diesel engine was used in the Indy 500.

Rockne Dies in Airplane Crash

On April 1, the entire country awoke to news that must have seemed like a terrible April Fool's joke: ROCKNE DEAD screamed the newspaper headlines. Unfortunately, it was true.

University of Notre Dame coach Knute Rockne, one of the most celebrated figures of the past decade, died the day before in a plane crash in Kansas. Rockne, 42, and seven others had boarded a plane in Kansas City that was bound, after a

Coaching Legend   *The death of Notre Dame coach Knute Rockne (left) stunned the sports world.*

few stops, for Los Angeles. Trans-Continental & Western Airways flight 599 took off 45 minutes late and into a steady and chilly drizzle. Less than an hour later, its engine sputtering, one wing gone and a trail of black smoke following it, the plane crashed into a wheat field outside the town of Bazaar, Kansas. Everyone aboard the plane died. Rockne was reportedly found clutching a rosary in his hands.

It was inconceivable that a man of Rockne's charisma and vigor was gone. His Notre Dame football team had just wrapped up its second consecutive undefeated season and his nationwide popularity, which ranked with Babe Ruth and Bobby Jones, had never been greater. Few people—Ruth, Jones and Red Grange among them—could appreciate the extraordinary demands made on Rockne's

1931

time. He picked his off-season engagements prudently. He was traveling to Los Angeles, for instance, so he could take part in a football demonstration film. For just a few days' work, Rockne was offered $75,000, which was more than he had earned coaching football for 13 seasons in South Bend, Indiana.

Two days after the crash, a train was carrying Rockne's body back to Chicago from Kansas City. It was met at Dearborn Station by more than 10,000 people. More than 1,600 newspapers printed editorials about Rockne's life. His funeral, on campus at Notre Dame's Sacred Heart Church, was broadcast live in North America, South America, Europe, and Asia.

Cards vs. Elephants *The Philadelphia Athletics used a white elephant as one of its symbols based on something an opposing manager had said years earlier.*

Rockne's death, like the Great Depression in which the nation found itself, was a signal that the carefree Roaring Twenties were over. A darker, grimmer period was ahead. Beside giving college football, its most memorable exhortation ("Win one for the Gipper!", see page 50), Rockne died with a career coaching record of 105–12–5. In terms of winning percentage, that remains the best in the history of college football.

Grove Wins 31 in '31

Robert Moses "Lefty" Grove was celebrated for throwing heat and feared for making teammates, opponents, and umpires feel it. The 6-foot-3, 190-pound baseball pitcher was one of the hardest throwers of all time. And as well as the Philadelphia Athletics' ace could throw a fastball, he threw temper tantrums just as easily.

Grove's teammates, as well as his mild-mannered manager, Connie Mack, were willing to withstand his wrath. His arm was that spectacular. In 1931, Grove led the American League in strikeouts for the seventh consecutive season. He had only been in the major leagues for seven seasons, yet he led the league in ERA for the fourth time. (When he retired, he had led the A.L. for nine years; no other pitcher ever did that more than five times.)

Most remarkably, however, was Grove's won-lost record. He went 31–4 in 1931. Granted, these Athletics, who compiled streaks of 13 and 17 wins on the road to their third straight A.L. pennant, were a special ballclub. But nobody wanted to win more than Grove.

That is why, although Grove won 31 in '31 (only once since has anyone won that many: Denny McLain of the Detroit Tigers went 31–6 in 1968), plus a pair of World Series games, his most memorable outing was a loss. On August 23, Grove took the mound in St. Louis against the hapless Browns in search of his 17th consecutive victory. Two pitchers, the superb Walter Johnson and Smokey Joe Wood, had won 16 straight, but no one had ever won 17 games in a row.

The Athletics were without left fielder Al Simmons, a future Hall of Famer with a career .334 batting average. Simmons took the day off to consult a doctor. Grove, known as much for his fiery competitive nature as for his great pitching skill, may have quietly seethed that Simmons was not in the lineup (he was not even in St. Louis), but he turned crimson when Simmons's replacement, Johnny Moore, misplayed a ball hit to left field that scored the game's only run. Grove pitched well, but the Browns' Dick Coffman pitched better, throwing a three-hit shutout. The Athletics lost, 1–0.

Grove won the Most Valuable Player award in what was one of the most outstanding seasons any pitcher has ever compiled. Besides attaining the position's unofficial Triple Crown (leader in victories, strikeouts, and ERA), Grove tied the record for consecutive wins with 16. He also won two World Series games, although the Athletics lost the Series in seven games to the St. Louis Cardinals in October. He did all that—but Lefty Grove never did forgive Simmons for missing that game against the Browns.

Just Like This, Boys   *Curly Lambeau helped start the Green Bay Packers, as well as the team's legendary success. He coached the Packers to three straight NFL championships.*

Packers Go For Three

Before the 1929 NFL season, Earl "Curly" Lambeau, who founded, coached and played halfback for the Green Bay Packers, wrote a letter to a young man named Johnny "Blood" McNally.

"Dear John," the letter began. "If you join the Green Bay Packers for the 1929 season, I'll pay you $100 per game." It included a postscript: "P.S. If you don't drink

65

1931

beyond Wednesday night before a game, I'll pay you $110."

McNally read Lambeau's letter, noting the $10 inducement to curb his carousing. McNally accepted Lambeau's offer to play for the Packers, but he refused, even though Prohibition (a 1919 law that banned the sale of alcoholic beverages) was still in force, to curb his drinking. "I'll take the $100," McNally wrote back.

With Lambeau and McNally in the backfield, plus mammoth 6-foot-5, 250-pound tackle Cal Hubbard on the line, the Packers won the first of three straight NFL championships in 1929. Championships were not decided by playoffs at this time. Instead, the team that had the best record at the end of the regular season was named champion. The Packers' three-year record from 1929 to 1931 was 34–5–1.

When the Pro Football Hall of Fame inducted its first class of 16 men in 1963, Lambeau, McNally, and Hubbard were all included (Hubbard later made the Baseball Hall of Fame as an umpire; he is the only person to be inducted into both Halls). Lambeau was pro football's first advocate of the forward pass. That type of offensive play was legal, but few teams used passes, preferring to run the ball. In 1931, the Packers scored 291 points, more than 100 points better than any other team.

Women in the Spotlight

Seventeen-year-old female pitcher Jackie Mitchell was signed by the Chattanooga Lookouts in June. They played an exhibition game against the New York Yankees. Mitchell struck out Babe Ruth and Lou Gehrig, although the wildness of their swings suggested to some observers that they were trying to make it easy for her. Mitchell's contract was soon voided by the Southern League in which the Lookouts played. Only two other women have played baseball for minor league teams: first baseman Julie Cocteau and pitcher Ila Borders, both in the 1990s.

In 1931, another female teenager, Mildred "Babe" Didrikson, proved herself a star athlete by setting world records for the 80-meter high hurdles and the baseball throw in the same afternoon. In the coming decades, the multi-talented Didrikson became the world's greatest female athlete adding success in golf and tennis to her track achievements (see page 68).

Award Season

Choosing the player of the year or athlete of the year is now an annual ritual in sports. Dozens of organizations, from professional sports leagues, sports clubs, and media organizations, choose "best" athletes in a wide variety of sports. ESPN, the cable sports channel, even puts its awards show on television—the ESPYs—attracting large audiences to watch the sports world's best.

The Sullivan Award had been established in 1930 to honor the top amateur athlete in the country (see page 61). Sensing a good thing, the *Associated Press* began naming its own athlete of the year in 1931.

The first *AP* Athlete of the Year was St. Louis Cardinals outfielder Pepper Martin. In the World Series, Martin sparked the Cardinals to a win over the

Other Milestones of 1931

✔ On July 12 at Sportsman's Park in St. Louis, the Cardinals and the Chicago Cubs combined for a Major League Baseball record 21 doubles in a 17–13 win by the Cardinals. The game was, naturally, the second game of a doubleheader.

✔ New York Yankees catcher Bill Dickey set a Major League Baseball record that has never been matched by playing an entire season without allowing a single passed ball. (A passed ball is a mistake by a catcher that lets a pitch get past him allowing baserunners to advance.) Dickey finished the year with a .996 fielding percentage.

✔ On November 21, the University of Southern California visited Notre Dame for a football game. The Irish of Notre Dame had a 26-game unbeaten streak and, despite the death of coach Knute Rockne, were 6–0–1 and had surrendered just 12 points all season. The Southern California Trojans, trailing 14–0 entering the fourth quarter, shocked the Irish with two touchdowns and a late field goal to win the game, 16–14. The rivalry between the two national powers has become one of the biggest in the nation and the two teams still play each year.

Philadelphia Athletics in seven games. Batting .500, the fiesty Martin set a record with 12 hits in the Series and stole five bases. Along with earning the first *AP* award, Martin also boasted one of baseball's best nicknames, given for his birthplace and his hustling style: Wild Horse of the Osage.

AP also named a female athlete of the year, a forward-thinking idea in a time when women's sports did not receive much attention. Swimmer Helene Madison earned the first award. She was the U.S. record holder in freestyle at every distance up to 800 yards, and would win three gold medals at the Olympics in Los Angeles the next year. Babe Didrickson eventually won the most *AP* Athlete of the Year awards with six (her first was in 1932). Basketball player Michael Jordan and golfer Tiger Woods are the only male athletes to win the award three times.

1932

A Pair of Golds

At the Winter Olympics in Lake Placid in February, Eddie Eagan won a gold medal as a member of the U.S.A.'s four-man bobsled team. Twelve years earlier Eagan had won a gold at the Summer Olympics in Antwerp in boxing. He was the first person, and remains the only American, to win gold medals in both the Summer and Winter Olympics.

The Winter Olympics this year were the first held in the United States. It was the only time in Winter Olympics history that the United States won the most overall medals.

Another Immortal Babe

On July 16 in Evanston, Illinois, Mildred Ella "Babe" Didrikson (1915–1956) destroyed the maxim that "there's no I in team." The event was the Amateur Athletic Union (AAU) Championships for track and field. The Golden Cyclones, a team sponsored by Employers Casualty Company of Dallas, where Didrikson worked.

Didrikson entered eight of the 10 track events on this afternoon. She finished in first place in five of the events—shotput, javelin throw, baseball throw, 80-meter hurdles, and long jump—and tied for first place in a sixth event, high jump. She finished fourth in the discus throw. In four events she set world records.

In all, Didrikson amassed 30 points, which was eight more than the entire 20-member squad of the second-place Illinois Women's Athletic Club.

It is no coincidence that the most outstanding male athlete and female athlete of the first half of the 20th century share the same nickname. Didrikson was called "Babe" because the boys in her neighborhood thought she batted like baseball superstar Babe Ruth.

The daughter of Norwegian immigrants, the 5-foot-5 Didrikson excelled at every sport she attempted. In 1932 she was named an All-American in basketball (her best sport—she reportedly once scored 106 points in a game) for the third straight year. She also was successful in baseball, bowling, swimming, volleyball, and tennis. Asked if there was anything that she didn't play, the sharp-tongued Didrikson famously replied, "Yeah, dolls."

Woman Warrior *Babe Didrickson (second from right) dominated the track events at the Summer Olympics. The inset photo shows a ticket from a rowing event at those 1932 Games.*

Didrikson did things her own way. Abrasive and aggressive, she alienated teammates and opponents alike, which may be why her one-woman team at the AAUs suited her best. Her attention-grabbing performance in Evanston qualified her for three events at the 1932 Summer Olympic Games in Los Angeles. She might have qualified for more, but the Olympics at that time only had three track and field events for female athletes: the javelin throw, the 80-meter hurdles and the high jump.

Didrikson won the gold medal in both the hurdles and the javelin throw. Her javelin toss, though unconventional (she looked like a baseball catcher trying to throw out a runner stealing second base), landed at 143 feet, 3 11/16 inches, surpassing the world record by 11 feet.

Didrikson's high jump of 5 feet, 4 15/16 inches put her in a first-place tie with fellow American Jean Shiley, which would have given her a track and field sweep. However, judges ruled that her method of jumping, in which her head

1932

cleared the bar before her feet did, was against the rules. She had to settle for a silver medal.

The high jump controversy in Los Angeles was symbolic of Didrikson's legacy. Nowadays, every world-class high jumper leaps the way Babe did. If Babe Didrikson was guilty of anything at the Olympics, it was being way ahead of her time.

Babe Ruth's Called Shot

When you look at the life of a legend, sometimes it's difficult to separate fact from fiction. This much is known for sure about Babe Ruth's historic called shot home run: It occurred on October 1 at Wrigley Field in Chicago. The New York Yankees were playing the Chicago Cubs in game three of the World Series, which New York's Bronx Bombers would sweep in four games. It was the top of the fifth inning on a sunny, brisk afternoon. Charlie Root was pitching for the Cubs and the score was tied, 4–4. Ruth had already hit a three-run homer in the first inning, and teammate Lou Gehrig followed with a solo shot in the top of the third. New York governor and Democratic presidential nominee Franklin D. Roosevelt was at the game.

What always distinguished Ruth, apart from his career statistics, was his flair for the dramatic. When Ruth approached the plate in the top half of the fifth inning, the Wrigley Field fans, who had heckled him all day, were full of bravado. Some fans taunted, while others tossed lemons. According to folklore, the Cubs bench was also razzing (teasing) the Babe.

What followed depends on whose version of the tale you believe. Root threw strike one, which the fans cheered. Ruth supposedly held up one finger and, according to Cubs catcher Gabby Hartnett, murmured, "It only takes one to hit it." Root followed with a pair of balls. Then a called strike. The count stood at 2–2. Wrigley Field was ready to explode if Ruth struck out.

Ruth stepped out of the batter's box. Raising his right arm, the Babe pointed. But where to? Was he pointing at Root? At the Cubs' bench? Or, as legend has it, was he pointing to beyond the outfield fence to indicate where he would hit Root's next pitch?

The big-swinging lefty launched that next pitch straight over the centerfield fence, a towering hit that measured 436 feet. It was the longest home run ever hit at Wrigley Field. It was also Ruth's record-breaking 15th, and last, World Series home run. But did he call it?

"He definitely raised his right arm," said Cubs shortstop Mark Koenig, who had been a former teammate of Ruth's with the Yankees. "He did not point to center field, but he did indicate he would hit a home run."

The one man who could definitively answer the question was not saying. "Why don't you read the papers?" Ruth said when he was asked if he had called the home run. "It's all right there."

Championship Gold   *More jewelry for the best team in baseball—the New York Yankees players each took home one of these rings for winning the 1932 Series.*

A footnote: True to his career-long role as the greatest second-fiddle in baseball history, Gehrig followed Ruth's memorable blast with a solo homer, his second of the game. The 1932 World Series will always be remembered for Ruth's called shot. Almost no one remembers that Gehrig set a Series record by getting nine base hits in four games. His average over the four games was .529.

The NFL's First Indoor Game

In surrendering their three-year reign as NFL champions, the Green Bay Packers learned that turnabout is fair play. The Packers were likely the league's best team in 1932, finishing with a 10–3–1 record (a .769 winning percentage). Although Green Bay had four more wins than any other team in the league, it did not have the NFL's top winning percentage. The Chicago Bears, who finished 6–1–6, and the Portsmouth Spartans, who were 6–1–4, both were at .857 (ties didn't count in calculating this percentage).

It was fitting that the Bears and Spartans, who had tied twice this season, should finish deadlocked. The league still had no official championship game, but in order to determine a champion it did arrange a "tie-breaking game" to be played in Chicago on December 18.

The weather did not cooperate with the NFL's plans for the game, however. Heavy snow and bitter cold created a sub-zero wind-chill, eliminating any chance of playing the game at Wrigley Field. Instead, the game was moved indoors, to Chicago Stadium.

No football field like it had ever been seen. Because a circus had just been held at Chicago Stadium, the field was a thick layer of dirt. Also, the size of the arena allowed only for an 80-yard field, plus smaller-than-regulation end zones. When a team crossed midfield, the ball was moved 20 yards back. The goal posts, which normally stand at the back of the end zone, were moved to the front. The field was also 10 yards narrower than the regulation 53 yards.

Late in the game it looked as if both teams were headed for a tie. The score was 0–0 when Dick Nesbitt of the Bears intercepted a pass and returned it to the Portsmouth 13-yard line. Chicago advanced

Rules Changes

Because frigid conditions forced this important NFL game indoors on an improvised 80-yard field, a new rule was born: The ball was to be placed not at the spot where the last play ended, but on a special mark. Two so-called hashmarks were placed near the center of the field, one for each yard line. Before the rule change, the ball was placed wherever the ball carrier landed. This had the effect of sometimes making the field almost lopsided, as players would be squeezed close to one sideline. Under the new rule, the ball was always moved back toward the center of the field, though no closer to the goal line. The new rule, permanently adopted in 1933 for all games, opened up the game offensively by giving each play a full field.

Also, league officials eliminated the rule that required a passer to be five yards behind the line of scrimmage. NFL fans today probably don't realize how good it was that the weather in Chicago was so terrible that day in 1932.

1932

the ball to the two-yard line. Everyone expected the Bears' Bronko Nagurski, a 6-foot-2 human steamroller, to carry the ball right up the middle. Instead, Nagurski, the most feared rusher of this era, faked a run and lofted a pass in the end zone to Red Grange, the former University of Illinois star (see page 30), now in the twilight of his great career.

Grange caught the pass, and the crowd exploded. The Spartans disputed the play, however. At this time the rule in football was that in order to attempt a forward pass, the passer needed to be standing at least five yards behind the line of scrimmage. Portsmouth argued that Nagurski had not been far enough

behind the line when he threw the pass. However, the play stood. The Bears went on to win the first unofficial NFL championship game, 9–0.

The following season the league eliminated the rule that required a passer to be five yards behind the line of scrimmage. This helped make passing a much bigger part of many team's plans. The NFL also realized that fans craved a champion and thus the league created its first official championship game. Indoor football became a regular part of the sporting scene with the opening of the Houston Astrodome in 1965, and with many other indoor arenas for pro and college teams since then.

Bears on the Prowl *Chicago Bears greats Bronko Nagurski (3) and Red Grange (second from right) are outdoors here, but played in the first indoor NFL game.*

Other Milestones of 1932

✔ In a controversial heavyweight boxing match, the champion Max Schmeling kept his title when opponent Jack Sharkey was disqualified for landing what the referee called a "low blow." Then as now, boxers are not allowed to hit an opponent below the waist. Sharkey later won a rematch against the German boxer.

✔ Purdue University was named national champion in college basketball following its 17–1 season. The Purdue Boilermakers were led by three-time All-American and National Player of the Year John Wooden. In the 1960s, Wooden led UCLA to the first of his 10 NCAA championships as a coach.

✔ On June 3, New York Yankees first baseman Lou Gehrig became the first player in the 20th century to hit four home runs in one game during a 20–13 victory over the Philadelphia Athletics. In the ninth inning, Gehrig launched a shot to deep center field that narrowly missed being homer number five.

✔ In international sports news, one of world sports' greatest rivalries got its start. Great Britain had introduced the sport of cricket to India, its colony at the time. The sport boomed in India and this year, the nation finally played its colonial master (losing by 159 runs). Today, "test" matches between the two countries are enormously popular affairs.

A Golfing Great

He was born Eugenio Saraceni in New York, but he gained worldwide fame as Gene Sarazen, champion golfer. He would win seven Major championships in his long career. In 1932, he had one of his greatest years ever. First, Sarazen won the British Open, setting a tournament record with a score of 283. Then, later in the summer, he found himself trailing at the U.S. Open. Sarazen already had earned a reputation as a great "finisher." That is, he excelled at charging from behind to win tournaments.

He certainly did nothing to change that at the U.S. Open. He rallied from behind to win with another record. His final round of 66 was called "the finest competitive round I have ever seen," by none other than golfing legend Bobby Jones.

Sarazen will be well-remembered for a shot he made at the 1935 Masters (see page 87). But he also made his mark on golf by inventing the sand wedge. The heavy, angled club is used by golfers to blast golf balls out of sand traps. The club has a heavy lower edge that cuts through heavy sand. "That club should have been called the 'Sarazen wedge,'" said Arnold Palmer.

Sarazen's Sandy *Champion golfer Gene Sarazen developed this club, which bears his name and is used by golfers to hit balls out of sand traps.*

1933

The Depression and Baseball

Baseball, the "national pastime," felt the aftershocks of the October 1929 stock-market crash, as did every other commercial enterprise. As a result of the sudden drop in the value of stocks and the solvency of banks, America entered a time of poverty and trouble called the Great Depression. Millions of Americans were out of work. With so little money, Americans had less money to spend on entertainment as opposed to, say, food.

Between 1930 and 1933 Major League Baseball attendance plummeted by 40 percent. For example, in 1930, the St. Louis Cardinals drew more than 600,000 fans. In 1932, that number dropped by more than half, and by 1933, only about 250,000 people came to their 77 home games. Their crosstown rivals fared worse. In 1933 the St. Louis Browns attracted a total of only 88,113 fans, or 1,159 people per game. Two years later St. Louis drew even fewer—80,922 fans.

Baseball fought its loss of revenue on every possible front. Commissioner Kenesaw Mountain Landis cut his own salary by $10,000. In 1933 Major League Baseball instituted the All-Star Game to stimulate fan interest. In 1935 some teams, appealing to a workforce that could

All-Star Bling *Players who took part in the inaugural All-Star Game received a commemorative ring like this one.*

74

The First All-Stars   *To help spur attendance during the Depression, Major League Baseball started the annual All-Star Game, which pitted these National League players against a similar squad from the American League. The A.L. won the first game 4–2.*

not readily take days off from their jobs, instituted night baseball games during the week.

Over the decade, Major League Baseball would average a paltry 6,600 fans per game. Still, not one of the sport's 16 teams folded during the Depression. By the decade's end, baseball had proven that it could hit any curveball the economy threw at it.

"I'm not worried about the game," New York Giants manager Bill Terry once said during the Depression's gloomiest

hours. "No business in the world has ever made more money with poorer management. It can survive anything."

The Rens' Amazing Streak

Pro basketball's pioneers did not, by and large, play in organized leagues in 1933. The National Basketball Association (NBA), for example, was still more than a dozen years away from its birth. Instead, pro squads barnstormed, traveling from town to town like a kind of hoops

Silver for a Crown *Philadelphia Athletics slugger Chuck Klein led the N.L. in homers, RBI, and batting average, thus winning the Triple Crown. His team gave him this trophy to honor his spectacular feat.*

owners of Harlem's Renaissance Casino. Douglas agreed to name his team the Renaissance to give the club publicity. In return, the Rens were allowed to practice and play their games at the popular dance club. Before long the Rens and the Celtics were engaged in a spirited, mutually respectful basketball battle of New York. Some games drew as many as 15,000 people.

Between the segregated teams, though, a hoops brotherhood blossomed. In 1925 the Celtics, the world's premier team at the time, had been invited to join the American Basketball League, a fledgling professional league. When the Celtics learned that the Rens had not also been invited to join, they declined.

The Celtics dominated the 1920s, once winning 44 straight games. By 1933, however, the Rens had overtaken their longtime rivals. Led by muscular 6-foot-4 center Charles Cooper and lightning-quick 5-foot-7 guard Clarence "Fat" Jenkins, the Rens doubled the Celtics' feat, winning 88 consecutive games. For the year they would finish 112–7.

It was the Celtics who at last ended the Rens' win streak, but only after the Rens had beaten them seven times in a row during the 88-game run. Basketball Hall of Fame coach John Wooden (b. 1910), who at the time was a member of the barnstorming Indianapolis Kautskys, remembers the Rens well.

"To this day," said Wooden, "I have never seen a team play better team basketball." Considering that decades later Wooden coached his UCLA team to an NCAA-record 88 straight victories and 10 national college championships, that is certainly high praise.

circus. The best of the barnstormers were the New York Original Celtics, all of whose players were white, and the Harlem Renaissance, or Rens, all of whose players were black.

The Rens were born in 1923. Bob Douglas, now known as the "Father of Black Basketball," made a deal with the

A Double Triple Crown

As easy as baseball's batting Triple Crown is to understand, it's that hard to accomplish. To achieve the Triple Crown in hitting, a player must lead his league in home runs, RBI, and batting average in the same year.

Since 1900, only 12 men have done it (Rogers Hornsby and Ted Williams did it twice). Only once, in 1933, did both the American League and National League have Triple Crown winners in the same season. Both players, coincidentally, played in Philadelphia.

Jimmie Foxx, who played first base in Shibe Park for the Philadelphia Athletics, is the more famous of the pair. In 1933 Foxx, who is best remembered for having slugged 58 home runs the year before, hit 48 homers, drove in 163 runs, and hit .356. As he had in 1932, Foxx won the American League MVP award.

His Triple Crown compatriot was outfielder Chuck Klein of the Philadelphia Phillies. Klein hit 28 homers, had 120 RBI, and batted .368. The short rightfield fence (280 feet) at Baker Bowl, the Phillies' home field, was an inviting target for the left-handed Klein, but he was more than a slugger. While Foxx led the A.L. in home runs a year earlier, Klein led the N.L. in stolen bases with 20.

Klein was the consummate five-tool player: He hit for power and average; he ran the bases well, finishing fourth in steals; he fielded well; and he had perhaps the best outfield arm in baseball. Klein registered 44 outfield assists in 1930, which remains the N.L. record.

In 1933, besides leading the league in the Triple Crown categories, Klein also led in total hits and doubles. For good measure, he hit for the cycle (a single, a double, a triple, and a home run in the same game) on May 26 against the St. Louis Cardinals. For all of that, Klein did not win the National League MVP award. Pitcher Carl Hubbell of the New York Giants did.

Adding insult to injury, Klein was traded to the Chicago Cubs in November. He is the only member of the exclusive Triple Crown fraternity to have been dealt right after his Triple Crown season.

A Classic NFL Championship

Before the 1933 season the NFL split its league into two divisions, Eastern and Western. The idea was that the winners of each division would face one another in a championship game. That came to pass on December 17, a foggy, unseasonably warm afternoon at Wrigley Field in Chicago in front of 26,000 spectators. Besides being the first official NFL championship game, the contest between the New York Giants and the Chicago Bears may have been one of the best.

For starters, there were six lead changes. After the Bears went up 6–0 on a pair of field goals, every score that followed put the scoring team on top: 7–6, Giants; 9–7, Bears; 14–9, Giants; 16-14, Bears, and so on.

There was some great trickery, too. In the opening quarter, all six of Giants center Mel Hein's linemates lined up to his right. That made Hein an eligible receiver. When quarterback Harry Newman took

1933

the snap, he handed the ball right back to Hein, who tucked it under his jersey. Newman dropped back as if to pass, then pretended he'd fumbled. Ten Bears fell for the trick.

"The idea," said Hein, "was that I'd just stroll to the goal line with the ball stuffed up my shirt. But after a few yards, I got excited and started to run." Bear safety Ken Molesworth spotted Hein and tackled him after a gain of 15 yards.

That trick play was planned. But in the fourth quarter, the Giants, trailing 16–14, scored on an improvised trick play. Newman handed the ball to Ken Strong on a left end sweep, in which Strong ran around the left side of his line. Hemmed in by defenders, Strong spotted Newman across the field but still back behind the line of scrimmage. Strong threw the football across the field to his quarterback, then sprinted for the end zone. "I was in the end zone waving to Newman," said Strong. Newman spotted Strong, and, for the second time that play, gave him the ball. Strong caught it as he was running out of the end zone and fell into the first base dugout.

Bears coach George Halas was furious. "Newman to Strong to Newman to Strong," Halas fumed. "Who would be foolish enough to dream up such a play?"

There were more highlights to come. Trailing 21–16 late in the fourth quarter, the Bears' Bronko Nagurski faked a line plunge (a headfirst dive into the line of scrimmage) at the Giant 33-yard line. Instead Nagurski jump-tossed a pass to end Bill Hewitt (who, incidentally, never wore a helmet). Hewitt ran a few yards and

then, just as he was about to be tackled, he pitched the ball backwards (called a lateral pass) to teammate Bill Karr, who ran the final 19 yards to the end zone untouched.

Chicago led 23–21, and still the dramatics were not done. On the game's final play, the Giants attempted their own pass-and-lateral play. Newman completed his pass to wingback Dale Burnett. The great Red Grange, playing in his final game, was playing defensive back for Chicago. Grange realized what the Giants had in store. He lunged toward Burnett chest-high and pinned his arms, not only tackling the Giant receiver but preventing him from making a lateral pass.

"It saved the game," said Halas later. "Red flung his arms around Burnett in a bear hug. It was the greatest defensive play I'd ever seen!"

The game ended with the Bears 23, the Giants 21. The first NFL championship game, as well as Grange's immortal gridiron career, were suddenly history. Neither would be forgotten.

Incident on Ice

Irvine "Ace" Bailey of the Toronto Maple Leafs and Eddie Shore of the Boston Bruins were two of the NHL's top performers when their teams met on December 12. Bailey, who led the league in scoring in the 1928–29 season with 32 points in 44 games, also led Toronto to a Stanley Cup championship in 1932.

Shore was a defenseman, the toughest and most talented the league had ever seen. In the 1927–28 season he spent a record 165 minutes in the penalty box.

Other Milestones of 1933

✔ The New York Rangers defeated the Toronto Maple Leafs to win hockey's Stanley Cup championship. The Rangers defeated Toronto three games to one.

✔ University of Chicago president Robert Maynard Hutchins forced the school's football coach of 41 seasons, Amos Alonzo Stagg, to retire. Stagg, who was 70 at the time, coached 14 more seasons at the University of the Pacific in Stockton, California. He added 60 wins there to bring his career total to 314, the second-most in collegiate history at the time.

✔ James "Cool Papa" Bell, the Negro League baseball speedster, stole 200 bases in 175 games.

✔ Jockey Judy Johnson, an Englishwoman, rode three winners in a single day on Oct. 7 at Commack, New York. She did it again on Nov. 12, and won two races the next day. Female jockeys were extremely rare in those days of widespread popularity for horse racing.

✔ Tennis player Helen Jacobs was the *Associated Press* female athlete of the year.

But he also scored like no other defenseman in hockey. In 1932–33 Shore racked up 35 points and won the first of his four Hart Trophies, the NHL's version of the MVP. To put his accomplishments in perspective, only Gordie Howe and Wayne Gretzky have won the Hart Trophy more times than Shore did.

Both Bailey and Shore, however, are best remembered for their fateful meeting on this night. The Bruins had a two-man advantage on a power play (when a player gets a penalty in hockey, his team must play with fewer men), and Shore was rushing up the ice with the puck. As he neared the Toronto goal, Shore was checked hard into the boards surrounding the rink by Maple Leaf defenseman King Clancy.

Either outraged or embarrassed by the vicious check, Shore rose to his feet looking for revenge. In the meantime Clancy had taken the puck and skated toward the Bruins goal.

Because the Leafs were at a two-man disadvantage, Bailey remained back on defense. Bailey's stick rested on his knees as Shore, who might have mistaken him for Clancy, plowed into his kidney and somersaulted him onto the ice. Bailey's head landed with a thud, fracturing his skull.

Bailey's teammate Red Horner skated over and whacked Shore over the head with his stick. Shore collapsed in a pool of his own blood. Shore recovered quickly, but Bailey was rushed to the hospital, where doctors said he would die within hours. Fortunately, with the aid of two surgeries and a nurse who slapped Bailey into consciousness by telling him that his teammates needed him, Bailey survived. But his career was over. Shore was suspended for the remainder of the season.

In the dressing room that night, after the collision but before Bailey lost consciousness, Shore approached him and apologized for his violent and unwarranted hit. "That's all right, Eddie," said Bailey, accepting the apology. "It's all part of the game."

1934

Leader of the Gashouse Gang

During baseball spring training in Florida, St. Louis Cardinals pitcher Dizzy Dean, whose younger brother, Paul, was a rookie pitcher with the same team, made this immodest prediction for the upcoming season: "Me and Paul will probably win 45 games."

Dean led the National League in strikeouts in each of the previous two seasons, but to many, Dean's boasts were just bragging. To which Dean replied, on many occasions, "It ain't bragging if you can back it up."

Dizzy and Paul did not win 45 games. They won 49. At the height of the Depression, Jay Hanna "Dizzy" Dean, the son of an Arkansas sharecropper, was a colorful breath of fresh air and candor. Dizzy finished 30–7 (he is the last N.L. pitcher to win 30 games in a season) and again led the league in strikeouts.

On September 21 at Ebbets Field in Brooklyn, Dizzy shut out the Brooklyn Dodgers, 13–0, on a three-hitter in the opening game of a doubleheader. Paul took the mound in the second game and pitched a no-hitter. "If you'd only told me you was gonna pitch a no-hitter," Dizzy growled at Paul (who won 19 games this season), "I'd have pitched me one, too."

Dizzy was the ringleader of the Cardinals, a fun-loving bunch who nicknamed themselves the "Gashouse Gang" (because they seemed more like a bunch of guys you might see hanging around a gas station than a team of ballplayers). In the World Series against the Detroit Tigers in October, each Dean brother won two games as St. Louis won the Series. Dizzy made headlines in one game when he was hit in the head by a throw while running the bases. He later told sportswriters, "The doctors X-rayed my head and found nothing."

When Dizzy died in 1974, *Los Angeles Times* sportswriter Jim Murray wrote, "Dizzy Dean. It's impossible to say without a smile, but then, who wants to try?"

Cunningham Runs Record Mile

It was easy to admire Glenn Cunningham for his middle-distance running ability. When Cunningham stepped onto the Palmer Stadium track at Princeton University on June 16, he was already famous for winning the Sullivan

Pair of Aces *Brothers Paul and Dizzy Dean teamed up to win 49 games and the World Series with the Cardinals. The inset photo is a brochure from a Dizzy Dean fan club sponsored by a cereal company.*

Award as the nation's most outstanding amateur athlete in 1933. In that year he won the NCAA mile as well as the AAU 800- and 1,500-meter races.

Perhaps more impressive was that he could run at all. Cunningham was raised on a farm in Everetts, Kansas, and when he was seven he and his older brother, Floyd, were involved in a terrible accident. It was Glenn and Floyd's chore to light their schoolhouse stove, and on a cold February morning in 1916, the stove exploded. The blast killed Floyd. Glenn's legs were terribly burned. Doctors feared he would never walk again.

Cunningham spent seven months in bed. His mother massaged his legs daily. Then came crutches. Then he began to walk without crutches, which led to an interesting revelation. "It hurt like thunder

1934

to walk," Cunningham later said, "but it didn't hurt at all when I ran. So for five or six years, about all I did was run."

Cunningham had turned his crippling condition to his advantage. In his final high school track meet, he set an national record in the mile (4:24.7). On this afternoon at the Princeton Invitational Meet, the 25-year-old set a world record in the mile, running the distance in 4:06.7.

In the decades that followed, many runners beat his mile record (including Cunningham, who ran a 4:04.4 mile in 1938). But none of them had come as far as he had to run four laps so quickly.

In His Shoes *Screwball-throwing Carl Hubbell wore these baseball spikes during a Hall of Fame career that was highlighted by the amazing 1934 All-Star Game.*

Screwball Comedy

Certain Hall of Fame pitchers are associated with a certain pitch. Nolan Ryan had his fastball, Gaylord Perry his spitball. New York Giants lefty Carl Hubbell threw a screwball, one of the hardest pitches to throw or hit.

Hubbell's screwball made him a hero to Giants fans, who called him "King Carl." The previous year he was named N.L. MVP while helping New York win the World Series. When he took the mound at the Polo Grounds (the Giants' home field) on July 10 as the N.L.'s starting pitcher in the 1934 All-Star Game, King Carl was cheered as if he were royalty.

With runners on first and second, no outs, now King Carl was about to face, in order, Babe Ruth, Lou Gehrig and Jimmie Foxx—the A.L.'s single-season home run record-holder, single-season RBI record-holder and reigning Triple Crown champ.

Ruth struck out on five pitches, looking puzzled as he took a called third strike. Gehrig struck out swinging on four pitches. Foxx fouled one pitch off, but Hubbell struck him out on three pitches. In the second inning King Carl continued where he had left off. He struck out Al Simmons and Joe Cronin to open the inning, before Bill Dickey managed to hit a sharp single to center. Dickey was stranded when Hubbell struck out the opposing pitcher, Lefty Gomez.

In two innings Hubbell faced eight future Hall of Famers (all but Heinie Manush). He struck out six of them. Although Hubbell had and would establish other remarkable pitching records, such as a

Other Milestones of 1934

✔ Horton Smith shot a 284 to defeat Craig Wood by one stroke to win golf's inaugural Augusta National Invitational on March 25. The tournament, which was started by the course's designer, golf legend Bobby Jones, eventually became known as The Masters.

✔ Boston's Fenway Park added a 37-foot left field wall that came to be known as "The Green Monster."

✔ Lou Gehrig hit for the Triple Crown, batting .363 with 49 home runs and 165 RBI.

✔ On December 29, promoter Ned Irish staged a college basketball doubleheader at Madison Square Garden in New York. More than 16,000 fans paid to see New York University defeat Notre Dame, 25–18,

Fenway Park's famed "Green Monster"

and Westminster College of Missouri beat St. John's of New York, 37–33. The big crowd proved the viability of college basketball as a spectator sport. The Garden became the sport's showcase for more than two decades.

---

consecutive scoreless innings streak (44 in 1933) and consecutive victories streaks (in 1924, 1936, and 1937), on this afternoon in front of his home fans at the Polo Grounds, Hubbell stamped himself as an immortal.

The Sneakers Game

The Chicago Bears entered the 1934 NFL championship game at the Polo Grounds in New York with a 33-game unbeaten streak and the first 1,000-yard rusher in league history, Beattie Feathers. Their opponent on December 9, the New York Giants, ended the game with something better: sneakers.

The temperature at kickoff for this rematch of 1933's inaugural NFL title game was nine degrees. The Polo Grounds turf was buried beneath a layer of ice—residue from the previous evening's freezing rainstorm. Giants president John V. Mara inspected the turf in the morning and informed head coach Steve Owen of the conditions. Owen, who had been told that rubber-soled sneakers would provide better traction than cleats, dispatched clubhouse equipment aide Abe Cohen to Manhattan College to obtain as many pairs of sneakers as he could get.

Both sides played the first half in cleats. The two-time defending champion Bears, on the strength of a one-yard touchdown run by Bronko Nagurski, led 10–3 at halftime. Back in the locker room, Owen directed his players to switch their cleats for sneakers.

The Bears scored a field goal to take a 13–3 lead early in the third quarter. From then on, however, the surefooted Giants scored 27 unanswered points. New York dethroned Chicago 30–13 in a game remembered today as "The Sneakers Game."

1935

300 m.p.h. on Land

Driving the cars that he always named "Bluebird," Sir Malcolm Campbell set eight international land speed records between 1924 and 1935. On February 7 of this year at Daytona Beach, Florida, Campbell, a former World War I pilot in the British Royal Flying Corps, established a world record of 276.082 m.p.h. That particular Bluebird was powered by a super-charged Napier aircraft engine.

But the 50-year-old knight yearned to go faster. Realizing that the hard, flat beach at Daytona did not give him enough space to break his own record, Campbell relocated his efforts to the Bonneville Salt Flats in Utah. There he fitted his new version of the Bluebird, which was 28 feet long, with a Rolls Royce R-type 2,500-horsepower engine that had an estimated life span of three minutes at top speed.

That was all the time Campbell needed. On September 3 Campbell gunned the engine and achieved a speed of 301.13 m.p.h., becoming the first person to break 300 m.p.h. The site of his record run became the home for many more land-speed records.

Jesse Owens's Finest Hour

When James Cleveland Owens (1913–1980) was nine years old, his family moved from Alabama to Cleveland, Ohio. There a teacher asked him his name. "J.C.," the boy replied. The teacher thought he said "Jesse," thereby giving America's greatest track and field athlete the name by which he would be known.

In May of 1935, Owens was a sophomore at Ohio State University. A few days before the Big Ten Championship track meet, he was horsing around with a few friends. He slipped and fell, severely injuring his tailbone. "My back was so bad the next morning," Owens recalled, "that they had to help me out of bed."

Three days after the accident, Owens, his coach Larry Snyder, and two teammates drove to Ann Arbor, Michigan, for the meet. They placed Owens in the car's rumble seat (a small, cramped seat at the back of some old cars) for the drive. Just before the meet Owens spent an hour in a hot tub to loosen up his back muscles. Snyder was prepared to withdraw Owens from the meet at the University of Michigan, but Owens kept repeating, "Don't worry, Coach, I'll be all right."

At 3:15 p.m. Owens, without even having stretched, lined up for the 100-yard sprint. He won in a time of 9.4 seconds, tying the world record. Ten minutes later, Owens prepared for the long jump. He boldly placed a handkerchief at the distance of 26 feet 2 inches, which was the world record. Then he jumped 26 feet 8 inches, shattering the world record by half a foot.

At 3:34 p.m. he ran the 220-yard sprint in 20.3 seconds, breaking the world record by three-tenths of a second. Finally, at 4 p.m., he ran the 220-yard hurdles in 22.6 seconds, becoming the first human to eclipse 23 seconds in that event.

In less than an hour, Jesse Owens broke three significant track and field world records and tied a fourth. Imagine what he might have done if he were healthy that day!

The Alabama Antelope

Even though he caught two touchdown passes in the University of Alabama's 29–13 Rose Bowl victory over Stanford on New Year's Day, little was known about Don Hutson when he made his Green Bay Packers football debut on September 22.

The "Alabama Antelope," as he was known, had not played in the Packers' season-opener. Green Bay coach Curly Lambeau was saving Hutson as his secret weapon for that afternoon's contest with the mighty Chicago Bears. When Hutson arrived in the league, the pass was still a primitive and seldom-used play. Ends (as receivers were called then) did not run specific pass patterns. If a team at-

Record-Setting Receiver *Don Hutson of the Green Bay Packers set records for receptions and touchdowns that stood for decades.*

Racing Across the Salt Flats   *Sir Malcolm Campbell's Bluebird was a record-setter in 1935, but today's rocket-powered cars travel at almost Mach 1 (about 750 m.p.h.), and would leave it in the dust. (See the story on page 84.)*

tempted 10 passes per game, that was a lot. By revolutionizing his position of end, or receiver, Hutson, who became the league's most dominant player over the next decade, changed the way football was played.

He did not wait long to get started. On the Packers' first play from scrimmage, from their own 17-yard line, Hutson lined up wide left. Arnold Herber dropped back to pass and threw the football as far as he could. Hutson, who was sprinting down the middle of the field, outran Bears defensive back Beattie Feathers, who was a speedster himself. Hutson glided under it, cradled the pass, and raced to the end zone untouched. The Packers beat the Bears 7–0, and a passing revolution began. The skill of players like Hutson and Sammy Baugh (see page 94) showed that air power would be the way to NFL success.

Berwanger Wins First Heisman Trophy

In November University of Chicago halfback Jay Berwanger received a telegram from New York's Downtown Athletic Club (DAC). The telegram informed Berwanger that he had been awarded the first DAC Trophy for being the "most valuable football player east of the Mississippi." The telegram also said the club wished to fly Berwanger to New York for the awards ceremony.

"It wasn't really a big deal when I got it," Berwanger said years later. "I was more excited about the trip than the trophy because it was my first flight."

The Dubuque, Iowa, native was known as "The One-Man Team." Besides playing halfback for Chicago's Maroons, Berwanger started as a safety on defense, and he handled the punting and kicking chores as well as returned punts and kickoffs. In 23 of his 24 career varsity games, he played all 60 minutes.

In his final game, against Illinois, Berwanger turned in a stellar performance. With the Maroons trailing Illinois 6–0 with less than a minute to play, Berwanger caught a punt at midfield and went around, over and through defenders before being tackled at the Illinois one-yard line. On the next play he carried the ball himself for a touchdown, then kicked the extra point for a 7–6 Chicago victory.

Although Berwanger went on to become the first pick in the first NFL draft in 1936, he never played a single down in the NFL, opting instead for a lucrative business career.

In 1936 the DAC Trophy became the Heisman Trophy, still awarded annually to the most outstanding college football player in the nation. The figure on the

JAY BERWANGER *Halfback*

ALL AMERICAN

Never a Pro *This commemorative football card, issued in the 1980s, featured the No. 1 draft pick who never played in the NFL.*

trophy is an image of Berwanger. But he cherished the memory of playing football far more than he did the trophy itself. "I ended up giving the thing to an aunt of mine," Berwanger said, "and she used it for a doorstop for 10 years."

Other Milestones of 1935

✔ Gene Sarazen hit his ball into the cup on his second shot on Augusta's 485-yard 15th hole, scoring a rare double eagle at golf's second annual Masters Tournament on April 7. Sarazen's miraculous shot helped him tie Craig Wood in the final round. The next day, Sarazen won a 36-hole playoff by five strokes.

✔ The all-white Boston Celtics played the all-black Harlem Globetrotters in basketball. With two minutes remaining and the score tied 32–32, the Celtics walked off the court rather than risk a possible defeat.

✔ On May 24 at Crosley Field in Cincinnati, the Reds hosted the Philadelphia Phillies in Major League Baseball's first night game. President Franklin D. Roosevelt threw the switch from the White House to turn on the lights. The Reds beat the Phillies, 2–1.

✔ On May 25 Babe Ruth, 40 years old and playing for the Boston Braves, belted three home runs out of Forbes Field in Pittsburgh. He became the first person to have three-homer games in both leagues. It was the 714th and final home run of Ruth's magnificent career.

1936

Schmeling KOs Louis

Since turning pro in 1934, Detroit heavyweight boxer Joe Louis had won all 27 of his fights, 23 by knockout. So stunning was Louis's right fist that the African-American boxer was nicknamed the "Brown Bomber." He dispatched all of his opponents, two of them former heavyweight champions, with such ease and regularity, that they were given their own nicknames: the "Bum of the Month Club."

On June 19 Louis, only 22 years old, stepped into the ring at Yankee Stadium to face former world champ Max Schmeling, 30, of Germany for a non-title bout. Louis appeared both intimidating and indestructible, but Schmeling hinted to reporters before the fight that he had spotted a chink in the Brown Bomber's armor.

Schmeling did not disclose his secret. He chose to reveal it to Louis first. In the fourth round Louis lowered his left shoulder, leaving his chin open for a right-hand counterpunch. Schmeling floored Louis. Eight rounds later the Brown Bomber had suffered his first professional defeat, by knockout.

Schmeling, who planned to fly back home after the fight in the dirigible Hindenberg, assessed his foe harshly after the fight. "He fought like an amateur," said Schmeling. "This is no man who could ever be champion." Find out Louis' answer for Schmeling on page 96.

The "Black Auxiliaries"

Tensions were high between the United States and Germany, the host of the Summer Olympics, when the Games got under way in Berlin on August 2. German Chancellor Adolf Hitler intended the Olympics to be a showcase for his theory of a "master race" of Aryan white people. The U.S. had 10 African Americans on its 66-person track and field team.

"The Black Auxiliaries!" the Nazi newspaper *Der Angriff* derisively labeled sprinter Jesse Owens and his nine black teammates. The Nazis believed that these "black auxiliaries" were of an inferior race and that it was a sign of American decay that the U.S. would choose to have black athletes represent the nation. Hitler and his Nazi supporters hoped the Olympics would help prove their racial ideas.

However, in front of 110,000 fans at the Reich Sports Field Stadium on the opening day Cornelius Johnson, who was

Triumph in Berlin *While loser Luz Long does a Nazi salute, champion Jesse Owens salutes the U.S. flag.*

black, won the gold medal in the high jump with a leap of 6 feet, 7 7/8 inches—a new Olympic record.

Nazi doctrine suffered another blow the following afternoon. Jesse Owens, running in front of Hitler and other proponents of the "master race," including Hermann Goering, Joseph Goebbels, and Heinrich Himmler, won the 100-meter sprint in 10.3 seconds. His time would

1936

Star Shooter *Hank Luisetti's one-handed shot revolutionized basketball.*

The dominance of Owens and the "black auxiliaries" was the story of Berlin. Between them, the 10 athletes earned eight gold, three silver, and two bronze medals. No other nation, nor their 56 white teammates, racked up as many points in track and field in Berlin as they did.

(In an interesting sidelight to the Olympic story, sprinter Marty Glickman, later a longtime sports broadcaster in New York, also made the Olympic team, but was pulled out of the relay event because of German objections to his being Jewish.)

Luisetti's One-Handed Revolution

Hank Luisetti sat in the stands at the Berlin Olympics and marveled at what he saw. Jesse Owens, on the greatest stage his sport could provide, had revolutionized it. Five months later at Madison Square Garden in New York—the greatest stage in basketball—Luisetti revolutionized his own sport.

Like Owens, Luisetti's real first name (Angelo) was not the one he was known by. Growing up in San Francisco, the son of Italian immigrants, Luisetti called himself "Hank." Luisetti was a skinny kid and lacked the strength to shoot a basketball in the accepted manner, which was a two-handed set shot. "I couldn't reach the basket," he explained, "so I just started throwing the ball with one hand."

Luisetti's odd style looked strange, but it worked for him. As he grew, he continued to use his one-handed running shot. He also grew to be 6-foot-3 and had an innate knack for playing the game.

have been an Olympic record if not for a strong tail wind. In the days that followed, Owens set an Olympic record of 26 feet, 31/64 inches in winning the long jump and another record in the 200-meter race, which he won in 23.7 seconds.

A few days after that, Owens ran the first leg of the U.S.A.'s gold-medal-winning 400-meter relay team. Owens' then-unprecedented four gold medals may still be the most impressive performance in Olympic track and field history. Owens not only defeated his competitors, he defeated Nazi racism. How must Hitler have felt as the Reich Field crowd cheered the champion's name over and over?

He enrolled at Stanford University where, playing for the freshman team, he averaged 20.3 points per game in an era when teams rarely scored more than 40 points in an entire game.

On December 30 Stanford and its inventor of the running one-handed shot traveled across the country to play at a sold-out Madison Square Garden in New York. The opponent was Long Island University. The Long Island Blackbirds, a powerhouse team coached by Hall of Famer Clair Bee, had won 43 straight games, but they had never seen anything like Luisetti. The Stanford junior dribbled behind his back. He looked one way and passed the other. And he shot that maddening running one-hander.

Luisetti scored 15 points as Stanford ended LIU's streak, 45–31. At the end of the game the partisan LIU crowd, who knew quality basketball play when they saw it, gave Luisetti and his team a standing ovation.

Other Milestones of 1936

✔ On February 8 Heisman Trophy winner Jay Berwanger was made the first pick in the inaugural NFL draft. The Philadelphia Eagles selected Berwanger, then traded his rights to the Chicago Bears. Berwanger met with Bears owner George Halas, requesting a no-cut, two-year contract worth $25,000. Halas promptly ended the meeting. Berwanger never played in the NFL.

✔ The Baseball Hall of Fame opened in Cooperstown, New York, inducting its charter class: pitchers Walter Johnson and Christy Mathewson, outfielders Ty Cobb and Babe Ruth, and shortstop Honus Wagner. The Hall of Fame building itself would not open until 1939.

✔ Californian Louis Meyer won his third Indianapolis

World Series Program

500 in nine years on May 30, averaging a record speed of 109.069 m.p.h.

✔ On August 23 Cleveland Indians rookie pitcher Bob Feller made his first start a memorable one, striking out 15 St. Louis Browns—one shy of the American League record, in a 4–1 victory. On September 10 Feller struck out an A.L.-record 17 (matching his age) in a 5–2 win against the Philadelphia Athletics.

✔ On March 24 the Detroit Red Wings and Montreal Maroons played the longest hockey game in NHL history. After three periods and five overtime periods, not only were both teams tied, they also were scoreless. Finally, in the 16th minute of the sixth overtime, Detroit rookie Mud Bruneteau scored, mercifully bringing the 176-minute game to an end.

1937

Triple Crown for War Admiral

In 1920 Samuel Riddle, who owned the magnificent thoroughbred horse Man O' War, did not like racing his horses beyond the East Coast. Thus, when Man

An All-Time Champ   *The great War Admiral, shown here in a recent painting, was one of the finest race horses ever.*

O' War's finest offspring, War Admiral, stepped to the starting gate at the Kentucky Derby as an 8–5 favorite amidst a field of 20, he was breaking new ground for his family.

Man O' War had won the Preakness and Belmont Stakes in 1920, but never entered the Kentucky Derby. War Admiral finished what his dad never started, winning the Derby by 1 3/4 lengths. At the Preakness, the striking brown colt outraced Pompoon in one of the great stretch runs in Triple Crown history, winning by a head.

The Belmont was a coronation of sorts. Although War Admiral stumbled out of the gate, injuring his right foreleg, he won by an easy four lengths. The victory gave the mighty horse the Triple Crown, besting his famous father.

He raced three more times in 1937, winning all three races to finish the year with eight victories in eight starts. Although a four- year-old named Seabiscuit had captured the nation's fancy as a rags-to-riches top-money winner ($168,642), War Admiral deservedly was named Horse of the Year. The argument as to which horse was superior would be settled the following year.

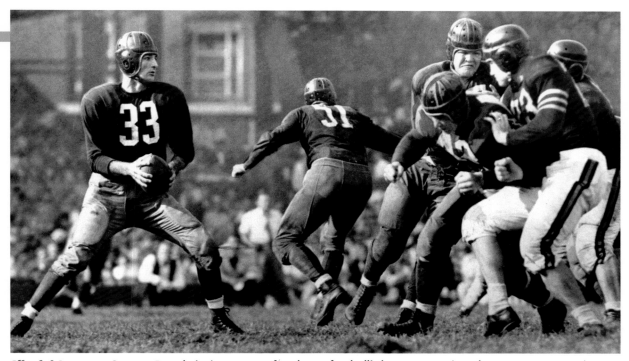

Slingin' Sammy   *Sammy Baugh (33) was one of early pro football's best passers (see the story on page 94).*

Budge and the Baron

In tennis, Don Budge of the United States and Gottfried von Cramm, a son of German nobility, enjoyed a rivalry of mutual respect that brought out the best in both of them.

The "California Comet" and "The Baron" had many memorable matches this year. On June 22 they met at the finals in Wimbledon, where von Cramm was runner-up twice in the last two years. Budge, only 22 but already ranked number one in the world, defeated the Baron in straight sets in the final, 6–3, 6–4, 6–2 (Budge also won in doubles and mixed doubles at Wimbledon that year).

A few weeks later, Budge represented the United States in a Davis Cup match against Germany. The United States had not won a Davis Cup (a tennis competition among national teams) since 1926 and, although Budge won his first singles match, as well as his doubles match with Gene Mako, it appeared the Americans would again go home empty-handed.

In the deciding singles match, played on July 20, Budge lost the first two sets to von Cramm. But the California Comet roared back, taking the next two sets by scores of 6–4 and 6–2.

Then it was The Baron's turn, as the German took a 4–1 lead in the fifth set. Budge summoned another comeback and, on his fifth match point, won the decisive set 8–6. After hitting his final winner, then racing across the court and lying sprawled on the Wimbledon grass, Budge looked up to see The Baron waiting for him at the net, wearing a smile.

1937

"Don, this is absolutely the finest match I have ever played in my life," said von Cramm, whose graciousness explained his popularity. "I'm very happy I could have played it against you, whom I like so much. Congratulations."

It was, in the eyes of many tennis observers, the greatest tennis match ever played. Two week later, as an encore,

Budge won all three matches he was involved in as the United States wrested the Davis Cup (an annual international tennis competition) from Great Britain.

The California Comet's brilliant summer was not yet over. On September 11 Budge and The Baron met one more time, in the U.S. Open singles final. Again, von Cramm took Budge to five sets before losing, 6–1, 7–9, 6–1, 3–6, 6–1.

Later in the year Budge became the first tennis player to win the Sullivan Award as the nation's outstanding amateur athlete.

Amazingly, Budge had an even more successful 1938 (see page 100). The Baron played no role in it, though. Von Cramm, who steadfastly refused to support Nazism and Adolf Hitler, was imprisoned in Germany by the Gestapo.

He Didn't Budge *Wearing the long linen pants typical of the era, Don Budge lunges for a return. The California-born player played a classic match against Germany's Baron Von Cramm.*

Slingin' Sammy Baugh

When Washington Redskins rookie Sammy Baugh reported to football training camp, coach Ray Flaherty attempted to prepare the two-time All-American quarterback for the NFL's higher standards. "Sammy," said Flaherty, "you're with the pros now, and they want the football where they can catch it. Hit 'em in the eye."

Baugh replied, "Which eye?"

The Texas native had a right to be cocky. On New Year's Day Baugh quarterbacked Texas Christian University to victory in the inaugural Cotton Bowl in Dallas against Marquette University, 16–6.

Baugh's first victory over an NFL team took place before he even played

Other Milestones of 1937

✔ On Memorial Day, May 31, at the Polo Grounds, the Brooklyn Dodgers roughed up New York Giants pitcher Carl Hubbell for 10 runs in the first game of a doubleheader, handing him his first loss in 25 decisions. Hubbell's 24-game win streak, the longest in Major League Baseball history, was over.

✔ New York Yankees centerfielder Joe DiMaggio enjoyed a monster second season, leading both leagues in home runs with 46. He also drove in 167 runs and batted .346. When his manager, Joe McCarthy, was asked if

Joe Louis

the sophomore sensation knew how to bunt, he replied, "I will never find out."

✔ Challenger Joe Louis knocked out world heavyweight boxing champion James Braddock in the eighth round of their title match at Chicago's Comiskey Park on June 22. Louis, at 23 years, 1 month old, became the youngest heavyweight champ in history.

✔ Montreal Canadiens center Howie Morenz died in March several weeks after fracturing his leg during a game. A blood clot from the injury was the cause.

a game for the Redskins. On September 1, in front of 84,560 fans at Soldier Field, "Slingin' Sammy" led the College All-Stars to a 6–0 victory over the NFL-champion Green Bay Packers in what was then an annual postseason exhibition game. The game's only score was a 47-yard touchdown pass from Baugh to Louisiana State's Gaynell Tinsley.

Later that year Baugh helped make passing fashionable in the NFL. In his first game with the Redskins, Baugh completed 11 of 16 passes to lead Washington to a 13–3 defeat of the New York Giants. Baugh passed—and punted (he is still the NFL's all-time leader in single-season and career punting average)—Washington all

the way to the NFL championship game.

The Redskins faced the Chicago Bears at frozen Wrigley Field on December 12. On Washington's first play, Baugh suggested a pass even though the Redskins were backed up to near their own goal line. This was unheard of; most teams only passed in desperation on third down and only after having crossed midfield.

Baugh launched a 42-yard pass to Cliff Battles, setting the tone for the game and, in all likelihood, a new era of offensive football for the NFL. Slingin' Sammy threw for 354 yards, including touchdown passes of 55, 78, and 33 yards. The Redskins beat the Bears, 28–21, to win the NFL title.

1938

War of the Worlds

Much had transpired, both in the boxing ring and around the globe, since Germany's Max Schmeling scored a 12th-round knockout of Joe Louis in 1936. Louis, the Brown Bomber, had won 11 straight fights, including the world heavyweight championship after an eighth round KO of Jimmy Braddock in Chicago.

Meanwhile in Europe, Adolf Hitler was herding Jews into concentration camps and invading Austria. While forging an alliance with Italy's Fascist dictator, Benito Mussolini, he was appeasing British prime minister Neville Chamberlain. Chamberlain returned home from Munich with a document that, in his words was, "symbolic of the desire of our two peoples never to go to war again."

Unlike Chamberlain, who was referring to World War I, Louis was itching for a rematch with Germany. The Schmeling loss had been his only defeat in 37 professional fights.

Meanwhile Schmeling, the world heavyweight boxing champion from 1930 to 1932, had made boastful—and uncharacteristic—references about being a member of a super race.

Thus on June 22, a year to the date after Louis had knocked out Braddock, he stepped into the ring at Yankee Stadium to box Schmeling again. This was more than just a heavyweight title fight. This was American democracy versus Nazi ideology. This was a worldwide radio audience of 70 million people. This was the very first time Americans, both black and white, rooted with every breath they had for the same man—a black man.

Louis, who had been given a pep talk by President Franklin D. Roosevelt, answered the opening bell bent on mayhem. Within seconds he hit Schmeling with two left jabs to the body, a driving left to the nose, and then a right to the jaw so devastating that it actually broke a small bone in Schmeling's spine.

The German fell against the ropes, virtually defenseless. Because of the spinal injury, Schmeling could not lift his left arm. A flurry of punches to the body and another to the jaw sent Schmeling to the canvas.

Twice more Schmeling fell. His coaches threw in a white towel, a sign of surrender, but the referee tossed it back and continued counting. Schmeling was counted out. Louis had knocked him

Germany Falls *The classic match between Joe Louis (left) and Max Schmeling had heavy patriotic overtones.*

down three times in two minutes and four seconds. In the process the Brown Bomber broke Schmeling's jaw and two of his ribs and laughably extinguished the theory of Aryan supremacy. He was hailed as "the first American to KO a Nazi."

Louis was always careful not to attach too much political importance to his victory. Schmeling, as history would show, abhorred the Nazi Party and Adolf Hitler. And, as for the United States being a true democracy, Louis, the grandson of slaves, knew that in 1938 that was a naive notion.

But, he said, "There's nothing wrong with America that Hitler can cure."

Still, the Brown Bomber's KO galvanized this country. It united people, white and black. Finally, it was a tremendous shot in the arm for a country that wondered whether or not it had the resolve for another war in Europe. "One hundred years from now," wrote Heywood Broun of the *New York World-Telegram* the next day, "some historian may theorize, in a footnote at least, that the decline of Nazi prestige began with a left hook."

1938

Homer in the Gloamin'

Chicago Cubs catcher Charles Leo "Gabby" Hartnett was behind the plate for Carl Hubbell's famous 1934 All-Star game strikeout bonanza (see page 82), the National League MVP in 1935 and on his way to the Hall of Fame when his most memorable moment came on September 28 of this year. Thanks to an eight-game win streak, the Cubs had climbed to within half a game of first place in the National League. Their opponent for the afternoon game was the first-place Pittsburgh Pirates.

When Hartnett, who had been named the Cubs' manager in mid-season, came to bat in the bottom of the ninth inning, the score was tied, 5–5. There were two outs and no men on base. Darkness and a haze were beginning to envelop Chicago's Wrigley Field. The umpires had already decided to call the game on account of darkness after the next out.

Hartnett fell behind 0–2 in the count. On the next pitch he smashed a home run into the twilight. The Cubs won, and in doing so overtook the Pirates in the standings for the first time all season.

Chicago clinched the pennant, thanks to Gabby's twilight homer. Its reward? A World Series date with the two-time defending world champion New York Yankees. New York swept the Cubs in four games, in the process becoming the first team to win three straight World Series.

Back-to-Back No-Hitters

The Cincinnati Reds' game against the Brooklyn Dodgers on June 15 at Ebbets Field in Brooklyn was a hot ticket. More than 40,000 fans, among them Babe Ruth, jammed the tiny ballpark hoping to see a historic first. They were attending the first Major League Baseball night game ever played in New York City.

Making this more interesting was Reds pitcher Johnny Vander Meer, 23, who four days earlier had no-hit the Boston Braves, 3–0. To this point only two pitchers had ever pitched two no-hitters in their careers, and neither had pitched both in one season.

Under the lights, the lefty had a no-hitter going through six innings. In the seventh he walked two, but escaped trouble. The eighth inning was routine. Vander Meer took the hill in the ninth with a 6–0 lead, just three outs from immortality.

Gabby's Gear   *Chicago Cubs catcher Gabby Hartnett, who hit a famous 1938 homer, wore this catcher's mask.*

The first batter, Buddy Hasset, grounded out. Then Vander Meer suddenly lost his control. He walked three straight batters, loading the bases and encouraging a visit to the mound by Reds manager Bill McKechnie. "Take it easy, Johnny," McKechnie told him, "but get the no-hitter."

The next batter was Ernie Koy. He grounded out. The bases were still loaded with two outs as Dodgers player-manager Leo "The Lip" Durocher stepped into the batter's box. The Lip had one ball and two strikes, one of them a dangerous flare that sailed just foul, when Vander Meer threw a fastball that appeared to catch the outside corner of home plate for a strike. But umpire Bill Stewart called it a ball. On the next pitch Vander Meer got Durocher to hit a pop fly to center field for the final out. Despite walking eight batters, Vander Meer became the first pitcher to toss consecutive no-hitters.

The first person to congratulate Vander Meer was the umpire, Stewart, who just two months earlier had coached the NHL Chicago Blackhawks to an exciting 4–3 Stanley Cup victory over the Toronto Maple Leafs. Stewart was the first American-born coach to win a Stanley Cup. Now he was congratulating another history-maker.

"If Leo got a hit, I was to blame," Stewart told Vander Meer. "I missed the pitch and the batter should have been struck out on the previous pitch." Vander Meer began his next start with three hitless innings for a Major League record of 21 straight innings without giving up a hit. No one has come closer than 13 innings since.

Double No-No *Cincinnati lefthander Johnny Vander Meer blanked first the Braves and then the Dodgers while racking up his unprecedented (and unmatched) back-to-back no-hitters.*

Seabiscuit

In 1938, a year of global turmoil, wrote author Laura Hillenbrand in her bestselling book, *Seabiscuit: An American Legend*, the number-one newsmaker wasn't Franklin Roosevelt or Adolf Hitler. It wasn't even a person. It was an undersized, crooked-legged racehorse.

What was it about this plain-looking runt of a thoroughbred that so captivated people, that made him, at five years old, when racehorses are past their prime, a national hero? As a two-year-old Seabiscuit had been lazy, needing 17 starts to win his first race. Then the colt was sold to a former bicycle repairman who hired a washed-up, blind-in-one-eye prizefighter, Red Pollard, as his jockey, and his fortunes changed.

The lethargic, down-on-his-luck horse rode trains from coast to coast,

1938

competing against all comers and in the process setting speed records at 13 tracks. As Seabiscuit's legend grew, his oats-to-riches story made him the ideal Depression-era hero, even if he was a horse.

"I had seen him before," wrote the legendary sportswriter Grantland Rice, "boxed out, knocked to his knees, taking the worst of all the racing luck . . . and yet, through all this barrage of trouble, Seabiscuit was always there."

In 1937 War Admiral, son of Man O' War, won every race he entered, including the Triple Crown. That same year Seabiscuit, grandson of Man O' War and a four-year-old, earned more money. War Admiral was named Horse of the Year, but Seabiscuit was the people's horse.

The people clamored for a match race. After two postponements, War Admiral and Seabiscuit met on November 1 at Pimlico Race Course in Baltimore on a beautiful autumn afternoon in front of a record crowd of 43,000. War Admiral entered at 1 to 4 odds on the 1 3/16-mile track, while Seabiscuit was the underdog at 2 to 1. After two false starts, using a walk-up start instead of the normal starting gate, they were off.

Seabiscuit flew to an early lead of two lengths, but War Admiral caught the five-year-old at the far turn. Neck and neck they raced through the backstretch. After a mile, they were still deadlocked.

The race came to the final 3/16 of a mile—and to which horse had the bigger heart. Would it be the Triple Crown winner? Or would it be, as Rice put it, "the horse from the wrong side of the track"?

Seabiscuit won by four lengths. He won in a track record time of 1:56.6, as the Pimlico crowd flooded onto the track to congratulate him. Seabiscuit was later named Horse of the Year.

Budge Wins Grand Slam

In 1937, Don Budge had had one of the greatest years ever by a tennis player. But in 1938, he did something that no player had ever achieved, and that only a few players since have matched: He won the Grand Slam.

Budge began the year by winning the Australian Open and then the French Open. Returning to the scene of his 1937 triumph, he captured the Wimbledon championship at the All-England Club. He did not lose a set at that event, finally defeating Bunny Austin in the final in three straight sets.

Championship Movie Seabiscuit, *a 2003 movie based on an award-winning book, was nominated for seven Academy Awards. Actor Tobey Maguire (above) played jockey Red Pollard.*

Other Milestones of 1938

✔ On New Year's Day Stanford University basketball star Hank Luisetti became the first collegiate player to score 50 points in a game as his team routed Duquesne, 92–27.

✔ Also on New Year's Day, University of Colorado All-American football player Byron "Whizzer" White threw an eight-yard touchdown pass and returned an interception 47 yards for another touchdown in the Colorado Buffaloes' 28–14 Cotton Bowl loss to Rice. Ten weeks later White, this time in a basketball uniform, represented the Buffaloes in the finals of the inaugural

Byron "Whizzer" White

National Invitational Basketball Tournament at Madison Square Garden. White, a future Supreme Court justice, scored 10 points as Colorado lost to Temple, 60–36.

✔ Glenn Cunningham ran a world-record 4:04:4 indoor mile March 3, but it is not officially recognized because it did not take place during a sanctioned meet. Nobody ran a mile faster, officially, until 1955.

✔ On the final day of the baseball season, October 2, Cleveland Indians pitcher Bob Feller, age 19, struck out a Major League-record 18 batters, but lost to the Detroit Tigers, 4–1.

The stage was set for Budge to become the first person to win all four of tennis' major events in the same calendar year. (The four tournaments are now often referred to as Grand Slam events.)

The final event on Budge's road to the Grand Slam was the U.S. Open, played in New York City. After sweeping to the final match without losing a set, Budge had to sit through six days of rain before finally taking the court on September 24. Facing fellow American Gene Mako, Budge won the first set, lost the second, then lost only three games in the final two sets to capture the title and the Grand Slam.

Since then, lefthanded Australian ace Rod Laver, in 1962 and 1969, is the only male player to match Budge. Maureen Connolly (1953), Margaret Smith Court (1970), and Steffi Graf (1988) have won the quartet of Grand Slam events on the women's side.

1939

The Birth of March Madness

As college basketball continued to grow in popularity, fans called for a national championship tournament. The National Invitational Tournament (NIT) was started in 1938 by a group of New York sportswriters, with top teams invited to New York to play for the title.

The National Collegiate Athletic Association (NCAA) wanted to get in on the act as well, and it started its own tournament. On March 27, the University of Oregon won the first NCAA Championship in an eight-team tournament with a victory over Ohio State University in Evanston, Illinois.

The NIT remained the premier college basketball tournament until the mid-1950s, but the NCAA became number one after that. This 1939 event was the forerunner of today's 64-team "March Madness" competition that galvanizes the sports world each spring.

The tournament today generates excitement around the sports nation. Millions of people enter contests to pick the winners, while television and Web sites attract huge audiences.

The Birth of Little League

Another part of the American sports scene was born in 1939. In Williamsport, Pennsylvania, businessman Carl Stortz wanted to provide young players with a more organized way to play baseball than in the dusty sandlots. He and some other local adults created Little League Baseball. The men organized players onto teams and provided proper uniforms and gear, as well as umpires and coaching.

The first Little League game was played on June 6, 1939. Lundy Lumber beat Lycoming Dairy 23–8. Over the coming years, the idea quickly caught on. Leagues were formed in other Pennsylvania cities and towns. In 1954, a national championship was created for players in the 11–12 year-old division. The Little League World Series has become a popular annual event.

Today, Little League Baseball is played in more than 80 countries, helping spread baseball around the globe. Plus, dozens of former Little Leaguers have become Major League stars. In addition, Little League Softball provides organized play for girls, which has led to United States international dominance in that sport as well.

Hug for a Hero *Babe Ruth (right) hugs fellow Yankees legend Lou Gehrig on July 4, during a ceremony held to honor Gehrig, who was stricken with ALS.*

"The Luckiest Man . . . "

On May 2, New York Yankees captain Lou Gehrig approached home plate in Detroit to deliver the team's lineup card. "Hey, what's this, Lou?" asked the umpire when he noticed that Gehrig was not listed in the batting order, as he had been every time for the past 2,130 games. Then the ump noticed that Gehrig, the Yankees' Iron Horse, was wiping tears from his eyes. Gehrig had taken himself

1939

out of the lineup "for the good of the team." The Yankees first baseman knew that something was wrong. A lifetime .340 hitter, Gehrig had slumped to .295 in 1938 and was batting a miserable .143 through the 1939 season's first eight games.

Seven weeks after ending his streak, Gehrig was diagnosed with amyotrophic lateral sclerosis (ALS), but at the moment no one knew what ailed him. Certainly the Iron Horse had played hurt before. But this was different. ALS, a usually fatal neurological disease, was—and still is—incurable. It is a measure of Gehrig's stature, not only in baseball but in the national spotlight, that ALS came to be known as "Lou Gehrig's Disease."

The Yankees designated a July 4 doubleheader with the Washington Senators as "Lou Gehrig Day." Gehrig's teammates, past and present, including Ruth (whom he had not spoken to in six years), as well as 61,008 fans, came on a gorgeous day to honor the man they called "the Pride of the Yankees."

After being showered with gifts and praise, the Iron Horse stepped to the microphone at home plate and delivered a moving speech, part of which included these famous words: "Fans, for the past two weeks you have been reading about the bad break I got. Yet today I consider myself the luckiest man on the face of this earth."

Gehrig, one of baseball's all-time greats, spent an entire career playing in the shadow of first Babe Ruth and later Joe DiMaggio. "Let's face it," Gehrig once said. "I'm not a headline guy."

On this Fourth of July, Gehrig was finally given his due. At season's end the Yankees retired his number 4, making his baseball's first retired number.

Also, the Major League Baseball Hall of Fame, whose building opened this year in Cooperstown, New York, waived its five-year eligibility requirement for Gehrig. Instead of having to wait the mandated five years after retiring to be eligible, Gehrig was voted into the Hall of Fame immediately.

Though he tried every cure known at the time and showed the same courage he had shown in crafting his streak, Gehrig died in 1941. He remains one of baseball's most-beloved figures.

The Dawn of Television

A New Way to Watch Sports   *The year 1939 saw a number of television "firsts," including many from the world of sports. In the coming decades, TV would have a huge impact on sports, too.*

Fifteen days after Lou Gehrig removed himself from the Yankees' lineup, his alma mater, Columbia Univer-

Other Milestones of 1939

✔ On April 20 Ted Williams made his Major League Baseball debut with the Boston Red Sox at Yankee Stadium, in a 2–0 Yankees' victory. It was the only game in which DiMaggio, Gehrig, and Williams all played. Williams ended his rookie season with a league-leading 145 RBI.

✔ Yankees centerfielder Joe DiMaggio, his batting average as high as .412 in September, finished the season batting .381 to lead the American League. The Bronx Bombers won their fourth consecutive World Series in October, sweeping the Cincinnati Reds.

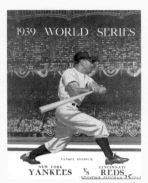

World Series Program

sity, played an historic baseball game. The Columbia Lions lost 2–1 to Princeton in 10 innings. More important than the score, though was the fact that it was the first baseball game to be televised. WSBX-TV in New York broadcast the game (even though most Americans did not own a TV set). The Columbia–Princeton game opened the door to sports television.

Other TV firsts of 1939:

- On June 1 the first boxing match was televised. Lou Nova defeated former heavyweight champion Max Baer on an 11th-round technical knockout.

- On August 9 tennis was first televised. The event was the Eastern Grass Court Championships in Westchester, New York.

- On August 26 WSBX-TV introduced television to Major League Baseball at Ebbets Field in Brooklyn. The Dodgers split a doubleheader with the Cincinnati Reds.

A Look Ahead

The 1930s ended with sadness as Lou Gehrig left the game, and found the world embroiled in the early stages of World War II. Sports would soon become a sidelight to greater issues, although they had a role to play in the war effort.

The flickering light of television soon had an enormous impact on every part of American life, but perhaps nowhere more so than the world of sports. The 1920s had begun to show that sports could play a major part in American entertainment, and that athletes were beloved as much—if not more—than other entertainers. That little glowing box in people's living rooms would soon prove this beyond a doubt.

The Golden Age of Sports in the 1920s and 1930s had given the sports world legends that are still talked about today. The impact of athletes such as Ruth, Owens, Grange, Didrikson, and others would be felt far into the future.

RESOURCES

1920s and 1930s Events and Personalities

The 1920s
By Erica Hanson (San Diego: Lucent Books, 1999)
Part of the Cultural History of the United States *series, this book explores the political, economic, and social mores of the 1920—from flappers to the stock-market crash.*

The 1930s
By Petra Press (San Diego: Lucent Books, 1999)
Another installment of the Cultural History of the United States *series takes the reader from the Great Depression to the beginnings of World War II.*

Jesse Owens
By Jim Gigliotti (New York: Sterling, 2009)
A new biography of this track star and American sports icon written for middle-grade students.

Sports Immortals
By Jim Platt with James Buckley Jr. (Chicago: Triumph Books, 2004)
This book features stories and photos of memorabilia of dozens of American sports heroes, including, from the 1920s-30s, Babe Ruth, Jim Thorpe, Joe Louis, Sid Luckman, Jesse Owens, and more.

American Sports History

Classic Ballparks
By James Buckley Jr. (New York: Barnes & Noble, 2005)
The history of six famous baseball ballparks is covered in this picture-filled book, including many teams that enjoyed great success in the 1920s and 1930s.

The Complete Book of the Olympics
By David Wallechinsky (New York: Viking Penguin, 2008)
An extremely detailed look at every Winter and Summer Olympics from 1896 to the present, including complete lists of medal winners and short biographies of important American and international athletes.

Encyclopedia of World Sport
Edited by David Levinson and Karen Christensen (New York: Oxford University Press, 1999)
This wide-ranging book contains short articles on an enormous variety of sports, personalities, events, and issues, most of which have some connection to American sports history. This is a great starting point for additional research.

ESPN SportsCentury
Edited by Michael McCambridge (New York: Hyperion, 1999)
Created to commemorate the 20th century in sports, this book features essays by well-known sportswriters as well as commentary by popular ESPN broadcasters. Each decade's chapter features an in-depth story about the key event of that time period.

Facts and Dates of American Sports

By Gordon Carruth and Eugene Ehrlich (New York: Harper & Row, 1988)
Very detailed look at sports history, focusing on when events occurred. Large list of birth and death dates for major figures.

Greatest Sports Rivalries

By James Buckley Jr. and David Fischer (New York: Barne & Noble, 2005)
A look at great American sports match-ups, both team and individual, many of which got their start during the 1920s and 1930s.

An Illustrated History of Boxing

By Nat Fleischer, Sam Andre, Nigel Collins, and Dan Raphael (Secaucus, N.J.: Citadel Press, 6th Edition, 2002)
This book takes you up to the current era of boxing, but it's also an excellent resource for information on some of the sport's earlier stars.

The Sporting News Chronicle of 20th Century Sports

By Ron Smith (New York: BDD/Mallard Press, 1992)
A good single-volume history of key sports events. They are presented as if written right after the event, thus giving the text a "you are there" feel.

Sports of the Times

By David Fischer and William Taafe. (New York: Times Books, 2003)
A unique format tracks the top sports events on each day of the calendar year. Find out the biggest event for every day from January 1 to December 31.

Sports History Web Sites

International Boxing Hall of Fame

www.ibhof.com
Legends, lore, enshrinees, and history of the sport that once riveted the American public.

Official League Web Sites

www.nfl.com
www.mlb.com
www.nhl.com
Each of the major sports leagues has history sections on their official Web sites. NBA.com is another, though that league did not get its start until later in the century.

Official Olympics Web Site

http://www.olympic.org/uk/games/index_uk.asp
Complete history of the Olympic Games, presented by the International Olympic Committee.

Sports Reference

www.sports-reference.com
By far the most detailed central site, including separate sections on baseball, basketball, football, hockey, and the Olympics. The sections include player stats, team histories, records from all seasons past, and much more.

The Sporting News "Vault"

www.sportingnews.com/archives
More than 100 years old, The St. Louis-based Sporting News is the nation's oldest sports weekly. In the history section of its Web site, it has gathered hundreds of articles on sports events, championships, stars, and more. It also includes audio clips of interviews with top names in sports from yesterday and today.

INDEX